Edited by LOUIS B. WRIGHT / *Director, Folger Shakespeare Library*
VIRGINIA A. LAMAR / *Executive Secretary, Folger Shakespeare Library*

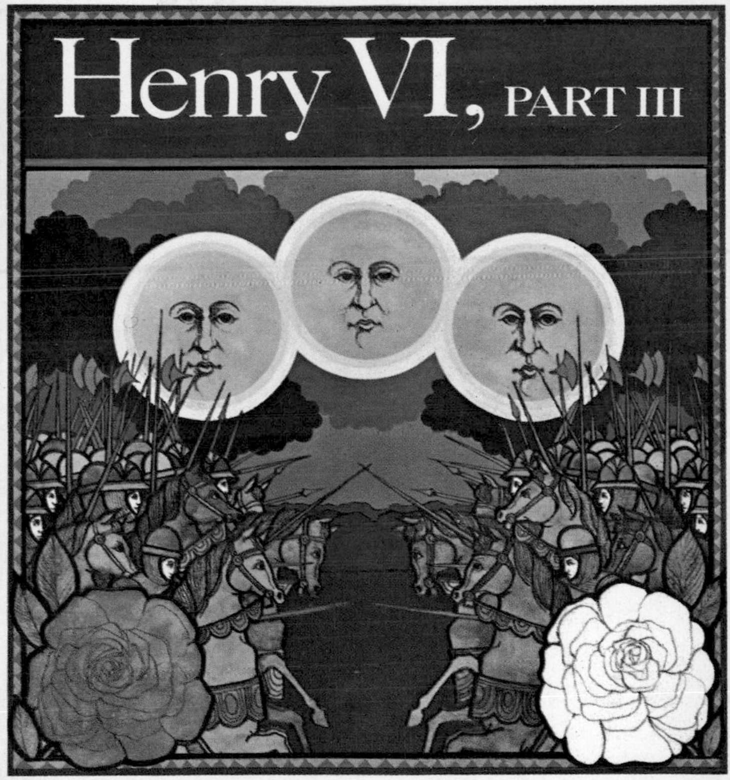

Illustrated with material in the Folger Library Collections

LOUIS B. WRIGHT, director of the Folger Shakespeare Library, has devoted more than thirty years to the study of the Shakespearean period. In 1926 he completed a doctorial thesis on "Vaudeville Elements in Elizabethan Drama" and subsequently published many articles on the stagecraft and theatre of Shakespeare's day. He is the author of *Middle-Class Culture in Elizabethan England* (1935), *Religion and Empire* (1942), and many other books and essays on the history and literature of the Tudor and Stuart periods. He has taught at the University of North Carolina, the University of California at Los Angeles, Pomona College, the University of Michigan, the University of Minnesota, and other American institutions. From 1932 to 1948 he was instrumental in developing the research program of the Henry E. Huntington Library and Art Gallery. Since 1948 he has been director of the Folger Shakespeare Library in Washington, D.C., which in that time has become one of the leading research institutions of the world for the study of the backgrounds of Anglo-American civilization.

VIRGINIA A. LaMAR, executive secretary of the Folger Shakespeare Library, has been on the Library's staff since 1946, and since 1948 has been research assistant to the director. From 1941 to 1946 Miss LaMar was a secretary in the British Admiralty Delegation in Washington, D.C., and in 1945 received the King's Medal for her services. She was coeditor of the *Historie of Travell into Virginia Britania* by William Strachey, published by The Hakluyt Society in 1953.

The Folger Library General Reader's Shakespeare

The Folger Shakespeare Library of Washington, D.C., is a research institution, founded and endowed by Henry Clay Folger and administered by the Trustees of Amherst College. It contains one of the world's most important collections of Shakespeareana. Its materials include extraordinary resources for the study of varied aspects of Western civilization from 1485 to 1715, and are not confined to Shakespeare.

Although the Folger Library's primary purpose is to encourage advanced research in history and literature, it also has a profound concern in stimulating a popular interest in the literature of the Tudor and Stuart periods. This edition of Shakespeare is designed to provide the general reader with a modern text that is clear and understandable, with such notes and explanations as may be needed to clarify obscure words and passages.

GENERAL EDITOR

LOUIS B. WRIGHT

Director, Folger Shakespeare Library

•

ASSISTANT EDITOR

VIRGINIA A. LaMAR

Executive Secretary, Folger Shakespeare Library

The Folger Library General Reader's Shakespeare

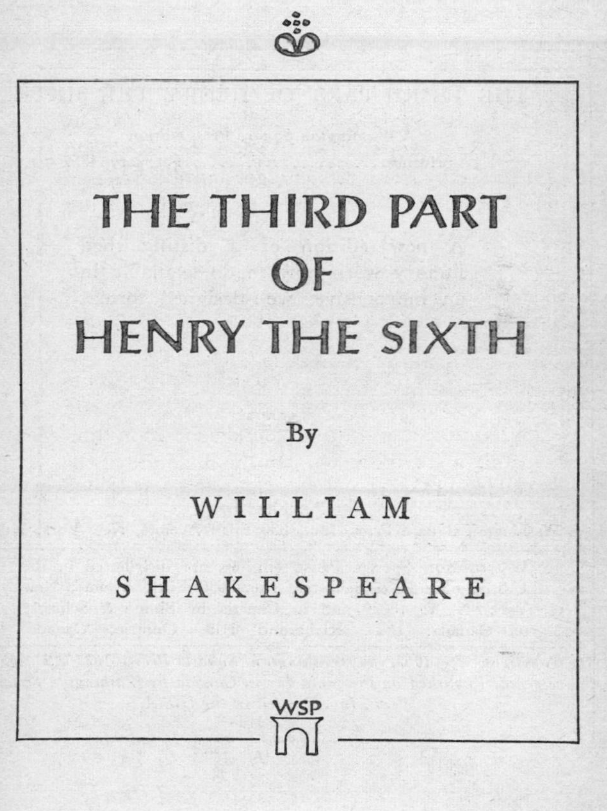

THE THIRD PART OF HENRY THE SIXTH

By

WILLIAM SHAKESPEARE

WSP

NEW YORK

WASHINGTON SQUARE PRESS, INC.

THE THIRD PART OF HENRY THE SIXTH

A *Washington Square Press* edition

1st printing.......................February, 1967

A new edition of a distinguished literary work now made available in an inexpensive, well-designed format

L

Published by
Washington Square Press, Inc., 630 Fifth Avenue, New York, N.Y.

WASHINGTON SQUARE PRESS editions are distributed in the U.S. by Simon & Schuster, Inc., 630 Fifth Avenue, New York, N. Y. 10020 and in Canada by Simon & Schuster of Canada, Ltd., Richmond Hill, Ontario, Canada.

Preface

This edition of *The Third Part of Henry VI* is intended to complete the trilogy of plays in which Shakespeare dealt with the Wars of the Roses. In the centuries since Shakespeare, many changes have occurred in the meanings of words, and some clarification of Shakespeare's vocabulary may be helpful. To provide the reader with necessary notes in the most accessible format, we have placed them on the pages facing the text that they explain. We have tried to make them as brief and simple as possible. Preliminary to the text we have also included a brief statement of essential information about Shakespeare and his stage. Readers desiring more detailed information should refer to the books suggested in the references, and if still further information is needed, the bibliographies in those books will provide the necessary clues to the literature of the subject.

The early texts of Shakespeare's plays provide only scattered stage directions and no indications of setting, and it is conventional for modern editors to add these to clarify the action. Such additions, and additions to entrances and exits, as well as many indications of act and scene divisions, are placed in square brackets.

All illustrations are from material in the Folger Library collections.

L. B. W.
V. A. L.

May 30, 1966

A Study in Character Contrasts

In *Henry VI, Part 3,* Shakespeare gives evidence of a growing interest in character analysis and character contrast, qualities that were to become increasingly significant in succeeding plays as Shakespeare matured as a dramatic writer. Although Part 3 is a jumble of historical episodes, it has more character differentiation than Part 2 or Part 1, which may have been written later. In Part 3, Shakespeare portrays King Henry as a more credible and realistic personality than he appeared earlier; and he begins the creation of Richard (later Duke of Gloucester and Richard III) as the monster of evil that he became. In the last half of the play, Shakespeare presents the pious and genuinely good King Henry in contrast with the evil Richard. Neither is a mere symbol, but both are endowed with qualities that reveal them as living personalities.

Part 3 covers the period from 1460 to 1471, when King Henry was murdered. The first Battle of St. Albans, when the Yorkists were victorious, had been fought five years before the play begins, although York and his followers are pictured as arriving in London fresh from the field. When the play opens, Richard, Duke of York, is revealed in the Parliament House in London toying with the idea of taking the kingship. Warwick the "Kingmaker" points to the throne, "this the regal seat," and tells York to "possess it." Warwick declares that he will see that no Lancastrian will ever move York from the throne that is rightfully his:

> Neither the King, nor he that loves him best,
> The proudest he that holds up Lancaster,
> Dares stir a wing if Warwick shake his bells.
> I'll plant Plantagenet, root him up who dares.
> Resolve thee, Richard: claim the English crown.
> [I, i]

York is seated on the throne when King Henry and his followers appear on the scene. In the argument that ensues between Henry and the Yorkist faction over who is lawfully King, Shakespeare reveals the constant theme of all three plays: the iniquity of rebellion against an anointed king, for Henry can find no proper answer to the charge that his grandfather, Henry IV, rebelled against Richard II and forced his deposition. York agrees to a compromise: Henry can remain as King, provided York and his heirs inherit the crown. This stratagem provides an opportunity for Shakespeare to introduce another element of sin which requires expiation, for York, persuaded by his sons, particularly the evil Richard, decides to break his promise to Henry. The wheel of Fortune turns, and, at the Battle of Wakefield, York and his party meet disaster. York himself is stabbed to death and his head is placed above the city gates of the town that bears his name. The theme of Nemesis overtaking evildoers runs through the play. In this episode, York's downfall and death atone for his perjury.

Henry VI, Part 3, provides the background for Shakespeare's more popular play, *Richard III,* which follows in historical chronology, even though Shakespeare may not have written the plays in strict historical sequence. In *Henry VI, Part 3,* Shakespeare begins to develop the character of Richard (later Richard III) as an archvillain. Early in the play he comes on the stage lugging the severed head of the Duke of Somerset and apostrophizes his grim trophy in these words: "Speak thou for me and tell them what I did." Richard's father, York, observes that "Richard hath best deserved of all my sons." Throughout the rest of the play Richard is portrayed as an evil genius, courageous but scheming. In persuading York to break his oath to Henry, Richard argues with Machiavellian casuistry:

> An oath is of no moment, being not took
> Before a true and lawful magistrate
> That hath authority over him that swears.
> Henry had none but did usurp the place;
> Then, seeing 'twas he that made you to depose,
> Your oath, my lord, is vain and frivolous.
> Therefore, to arms! And, father, do but think
> How sweet a thing it is to wear a crown,
> Within whose circuit is Elysium
> And all that poets feign of bliss and joy. [I, ii]

Already Richard is thinking of how sweet it is to wear a crown, and we later observe the way he plots his course to win that golden bauble for himself. When once more the tide turns and the Yorkists have placed Edward IV on the throne, Richard, now Duke of Gloucester, reveals the inner workings of his mind. Envious of the honor bestowed upon his elder brother, an honor that Edward has scarcely earned, Richard in a long soliloquy declares his determination to be King though he must wade through a sea of blood:

Ay, Edward will use women honorably.
Would he were wasted, marrow, bones, and all,
That from his loins no hopeful branch may spring
To cross me from the golden time I look for!
And yet, between my soul's desire and me—
The lustful Edward's title buried—
Is Clarence, Henry, and his son young Edward,
And all the unlooked-for issue of their bodies
To take their rooms, ere I can place myself.

Richard continues with a description of his crooked body, his withered arm, his hunched back, his uneven legs, and concludes that he cannot hope to bewitch any woman or deal in love's "soft laws." He must harden his heart and hew his way to the English crown with a bloody ax:

Why, I can smile, and murder whiles I smile,

. . . .

I'll drown more sailors than the mermaid shall;
I'll slay more gazers than the basilisk;
I'll play the orator as well as Nestor,

Deceive more slyly than Ulysses could,
And, like a Sinon, take another Troy.
I can add colors to the chameleon,
Change shapes with Proteus for advantages,
And set the murderous Machiavel to school.
Can I do this and cannot get a crown?
Tut, were it farther off, I'll pluck it down. [III, ii]

After this preparation, the audience is ready for Richard's bloody course. It is dramatically fitting that he is made the murderer of young Edward, King Henry's son, and, near the end of the play, of Henry himself.

After he has gained access to Henry in the Tower and stabbed him to death, Richard once more soliloquizes:

And this word "love," which graybeards call divine,
Be resident in men like one another
And not in me: I am myself alone.
Clarence, beware; thou keepst me from the light:
But I will sort a pitchy day for thcc;
For I will buzz abroad such prophecies
That Edward shall be fearful of his life,
And then, to purge his fear, I'll be thy death.
King Henry and the Prince his son are gone:
Clarence, thy turn is next, and then the rest. [V, vi]

With this picture of Richard already created, Shakespeare could do nothing else except make him a villain of consummate evil in the play that bears his name. Shakespeare was thus carrying out the

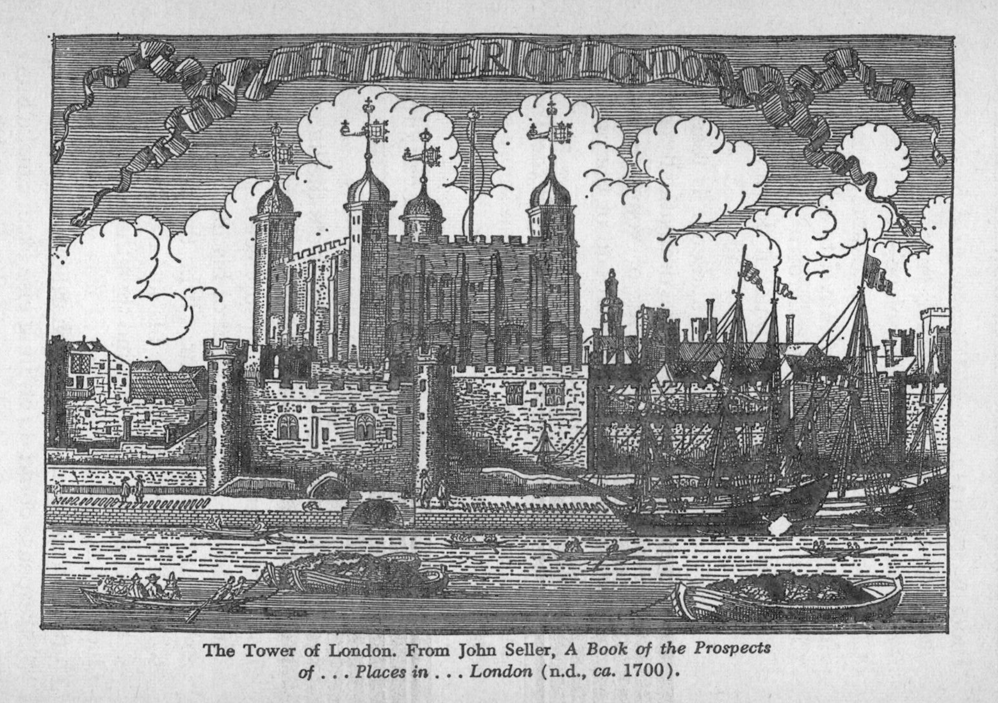

The Tower of London. From John Seller, *A Book of the Prospects of . . . Places in . . . London* (n.d., *ca.* 1700).

Tudor propaganda which required that Richard be made a devil in order to justify Henry Tudor's rebellion against him. In no other way could the deposition of an anointed king be justified in Tudor eyes.

While Richard increases in malevolence, Henry grows in dignity as the play moves to its fatal end. Earlier, Shakespeare had portrayed him as almost maudlin in his pious mumblings, but by the end of Part 3 he has taken on some of the tragic elements seen later in the chastened Lear. In the final scene between Henry and Richard, Henry shows no fear. He is reconciled to Fate, and he is aware of Richard's own destiny as he utters his last words in reply to Richard's boast that he was ordained to kill him:

> Ay, and for much more slaughter after this.
> Oh, God forgive my sins and pardon thee! [V, vi]

Though Henry achieved dignity in the end, his virtues were not sufficient to reconcile Shakespeare and his contemporaries to weakness in a sovereign. Among the lessons that the play drives home is the doctrine that disaster to the realm is inevitable when the ruler is weak and vacillating.

Other members of the cast of *Henry VI, Part 3,* show the playwright's concern with qualities and actions designed to emphasize characterization. Queen Margaret is a woman of iron will, as bloodthirsty as Richard himself when in pursuit of her enemies, a prototype for Lady Macbeth and other murderous women of Shakespeare's creation. Warwick is pictured as the proud "Kingmaker" who would brook no disgrace from the sovereign whom he had created in the person of Edward IV. On his return from the ill-fated embassy to France, he hails Edward as "Duke of York," and in reply to Edward's comment that he called him King when they last parted, Warwick replies with seething sarcasm:

Ay, but the case is altered.
When you disgraced me in my embassade,
Then I degraded you from being King
And come now to create you Duke of York. [IV, iii]

After a few more sarcastic lines, he plucks off Edward's crown. But Shakespeare makes Warwick pay with his life for his overweening pride.

This play is filled with action that suited with the tastes of the day. The Elizabethans enjoyed drum-and-trumpet drama, and Shakespeare provided enough noise and bloodshed to please the most sensation-loving groundlings. Yet *Henry VI, Part 3,* is more than a mere noisy chronicle play. It foreshadows the greater history plays and tragedies that followed. Shakespeare was rapidly working out his apprenticeship as playwright and could soon take his place as a master craftsman.

Shakespeare found his material for *Henry VI, Part 3,* in Raphael Holinshed's *Chronicles of England, Scotland, and Ireland* and Edward Hall's *The Union of the Two Noble and Illustrious Families of Lancaster and York*—chronicle histories that were a mine from which Shakespeare and other dramatists quarried material for plays. Shakespeare altered the

Henry VI. From a manuscript commonplace book by Thomas Trevelyan (*ca.* 1608).

historical material to suit his dramatic purposes, telescoping events and changing the time of action whenever conditions in the play required it.

Scholars formerly thought that Shakespeare in *Henry VI, Part 3,* revised an old play, published in quarto in 1595 with the title *The True Tragedy of Richard Duke of York and the Death of King Henry the Sixth . . . As It Was Sundry Times Acted by the Right Honorable the Earl of Pembroke His Servants,* but more recent scholarship has shown that the *True Tragedy* is merely a version of *Henry VI, Part 3,* probably put together from memory by actors who took part in the play. A similar version of *Henry VI, Part 2,* had been printed in 1594 as *The First Part of the Contention betwixt the Two Famous Houses of York and Lancaster.* Both of these quartos were brought out again in 1600. They were later printed together as one play in 1619. The best text, on which the present edition is based, is the Folio version of 1623, probably printed from a copy used in the playhouse. A few emendations are suggested by the quarto versions.

Scholars have also debated the question of the authorship of *Henry VI, Part 3,* and opinion has fluctuated as to whether Shakespeare was the sole author or whether he had the help of one or more collaborators. Current opinion leans to the view that Shakespeare alone was the author.

Although *Henry VI, Part 3,* was successful in its day, it was not one of the plays revived at the Restoration in 1660, and it did not attract attention again until this century. Recent interest in the history plays has given this play a new life in the theatre. The three parts of *Henry VI* were fused into two plays by the Royal Shakespeare Company at Stratford in 1964, with the second retitled *Edward the Fourth.* This stage version proved eminently actable. It has had a further stage life on television as part of the series called "The Wars of the Roses."

THE AUTHOR

As early as 1598 Shakespeare was so well known as a literary and dramatic craftsman that Francis Meres, in his *Palladis Tamia: Wits Treasury,* referred in flattering terms to him as "mellifluous and honey-tongued Shakespeare," famous for his *Venus and Adonis,* his *Lucrece,* and "his sugared sonnets," which were circulating "among his private friends." Meres observes further that "as Plautus and Seneca are accounted the best for comedy and tragedy among the Latins, so Shakespeare among the English is the most excellent in both kinds for the stage," and he mentions a dozen plays that had made a name for Shakespeare. He concludes with the remark that "the Muses would speak with Shakespeare's fine filed phrase if they would speak English."

To those acquainted with the history of the Elizabethan and Jacobean periods, it is incredible that anyone should be so naïve or ignorant as to doubt the reality of Shakespeare as the author of the plays that bear his name. Yet so much nonsense has been written about other "candidates" for the plays that it is well to remind readers that no credible evidence that would stand up in a court of law has ever been adduced to prove either that Shakespeare did not write his plays or that anyone else wrote them. All the theories offered for the authorship of Francis Bacon, the Earl of Derby, the Earl of Oxford, the Earl of Hertford, Christopher Marlowe, and a score of other candidates are mere conjectures spun from the active imaginations of persons who confuse hypothesis and conjecture with evidence.

As Meres's statement of 1598 indicates, Shakespeare was already a popular playwright whose name carried weight at the box office. The obvious reputation of Shakespeare as early as 1598 makes the effort to prove him a myth one of the most absurd in the history of human perversity.

The anti-Shakespeareans talk darkly about a plot of vested interests to maintain the authorship of Shakespeare. Nobody has any vested interest in Shakespeare, but every scholar is interested in the truth and in the quality of evidence advanced by special pleaders who set forth hypotheses in place of facts.

The anti-Shakespeareans base their arguments upon a few simple premises, all of them false. These false premises are that Shakespeare was an unlettered yokel without any schooling, that nothing is known about Shakespeare, and that only a noble lord or the equivalent in background could have written the plays. The facts are that more is known about Shakespeare than about most dramatists of his day, that he had a very good education, acquired in the Stratford Grammar School, that the plays show no evidence of profound book learning, and that the knowledge of kings and courts evident in the plays is no greater than any intelligent young man could have picked up at second hand. Most anti-Shakespeareans are naïve and betray an obvious snobbery. The author of their favorite plays, they imply, must have had a college diploma framed and hung on his study wall like the one in their dentist's office, and obviously so great a writer must have had a title or some equally significant evidence of exalted social background. They forget that genius has a way of cropping up in unexpected places and that none of the great creative writers of the world got his inspiration in a college or university course.

William Shakespeare was the son of John Shakespeare of Stratford-upon-Avon, a substantial citizen of that small but busy market town in the center of the rich agricultural county of Warwick. John Shakespeare kept a shop, what we would call a general store; he dealt in wool and other produce and gradually acquired property. As a youth, John Shakespeare had learned the trade of glover and leather worker. There is no contemporary evidence that the elder Shakespeare was a butcher, though the anti-Shakespeareans like to talk about the ignorant "butcher's boy of Stratford." Their only evidence is a statement by gossipy John Aubrey, more than a century after William Shakespeare's birth, that young William followed his father's trade, and when he killed a calf, "he would do it in a high style and make a speech." We would like to believe the story true, but Aubrey is not a very credible witness.

John Shakespeare probably continued to operate a farm at Snitterfield that his father had leased. He married Mary Arden, daughter of his father's landlord, a man of some property. The third of their eight children was William, baptized on April 26, 1564, and probably born three days before. At least, it is conventional to celebrate April 23 as his birthday.

The Stratford records give considerable information about John Shakespeare. We know that he held several municipal offices including those of alderman and mayor. In 1580 he was in some sort of legal difficulty and was fined for neglecting a summons of the Court of Queen's Bench requiring him to appear at Westminster and be bound over to keep the peace.

As a citizen and alderman of Stratford, John Shakespeare was entitled to send his son to the grammar school free. Though the records are lost, there can be no reason to doubt that this is where young William received his education. As any student of the period knows, the grammar schools provided the basic education in Latin learning and literature. The Elizabethan grammar school is not to be confused with modern grammar schools. Many cultivated men of the day received all their formal education in the grammar schools. At the universities in this period a student would have received little training that would have inspired him to be a creative writer. At Stratford young Shakespeare would have acquired a familiarity with Latin and some little knowledge of Greek. He would have read Latin authors and become acquainted with the plays of Plautus and Terence. Undoubtedly, in this period of his life he received that stimulation to read and explore for himself the world of ancient and modern history which he later utilized in his plays. The youngster who does not acquire this type of intellectual curiosity *before* college days rarely develops as a result of a college course the kind of mind Shakespeare demonstrated. His learning in books was anything but profound, but he clearly had the probing curiosity that sent him in search of information, and he had a keenness in the observation of nature and of humankind that finds reflection in his poetry.

There is little documentation for Shakespeare's boyhood. There is little reason why there should be. Nobody knew that he was going to be a dramatist about whom any scrap of information would be prized in the centuries to come. He was merely an active and vigorous youth of Stratford, perhaps assisting his father in his business, and no Boswell bothered to write down facts about him. The most important record that we have is a marriage license issued by the Bishop of Worcester on November 27, 1582, to permit William Shakespeare to marry Anne Hathaway, seven or eight years his senior; furthermore, the Bishop permitted the marriage after reading the banns only once instead of three times, evidence of the desire for haste. The need was explained on May 26, 1583, when the christening of Susanna, daughter of William and Anne Shakespeare, was recorded at Stratford. Two years later, on February 2, 1585, the records show the birth of twins to the Shakespeares, a boy and a girl who were christened Hamnet and Judith.

What William Shakespeare was doing in Stratford during the early years of his married life, or when he went to London, we do not know. It has been conjectured that he tried his hand at schoolteaching, but that is a mere guess. There is a legend that he left Stratford to escape a charge of poaching in the park of Sir Thomas Lucy of Charlecote, but there is no proof of this. There is also a legend that when first he came to London he earned his living by holding horses outside a playhouse and presently was given employment inside, but there is nothing better than eighteenth-century hearsay for this. How Shakespeare broke into the London theatres as a dramatist and actor we do not know. But lack of information is not surprising, for Elizabethans did not write their autobiographies, and we know even less about the lives of many writers and some men of affairs than we know about Shakespeare. By 1592 he was so well established and popular that he incurred the envy of the dramatist and pamphleteer Robert Greene, who referred to him as an "upstart crow . . . in his own conceit the only Shake-scene in a country." From this time onward, contemporary allusions and references in legal documents enable the scholar to chart Shakespeare's career with greater accuracy than is possible with most other Elizabethan dramatists.

By 1594 Shakespeare was a member of the company of actors known as the Lord Chamberlain's Men. After the accession of James I, in 1603, the company would have the sovereign for their patron and would be known as the King's Men. During the period of its greatest prosperity, this company would have as its principal theatres the Globe and the Blackfriars. Shakespeare was both an actor and a shareholder in the company. Tradition has assigned him such acting roles as Adam in *As You Like It* and the Ghost in *Hamlet,* a modest place on the stage that suggests that he may have had other duties in the management of the company. Such conclusions, however, are based on surmise.

What we do know is that his plays were popular and that he was highly successful in his vocation. His first play may have been *The Comedy of Errors,* acted perhaps in 1591. Certainly this was one of his earliest plays. The three parts of *Henry VI* were acted sometime between 1590 and 1592. Critics are not in agreement about precisely how much Shakespeare wrote of these three plays. *Richard III* probably dates from 1593. With this play Shakespeare captured the imagination of Elizabethan audiences, then enormously interested in historical plays. With *Richard III* Shakespeare also gave an interpretation pleasing to the Tudors of the rise to power of the grandfather of Queen Elizabeth. From this time onward, Shakespeare's plays followed on the stage in rapid succession: *Titus Andronicus, The Taming of the Shrew, The Two Gentlemen of Verona, Love's Labor's Lost, Romeo and Juliet, Richard II, A Midsummer Night's Dream, King John, The Merchant of Venice, Henry IV* (*Parts 1 and 2*), *Much Ado about Nothing, Henry V, Julius Cæsar, As You Like It, Twelfth Night, Hamlet, The Merry Wives of Windsor, All's Well That Ends Well, Measure for Measure, Othello, King Lear*, and nine others that followed before Shakespeare retired completely, about 1613.

In the course of his career in London, he made enough money to enable him to retire to Stratford with a competence. His purchase on May 4, 1597, of New Place, then the second-largest dwelling in Stratford, "a pretty house of brick and timber," with a handsome garden, indicates his increasing prosperity. There his wife and children lived while he busied himself in the London theatres. The summer before he acquired New Place, his life was darkened by the death of his only son, Hamnet, a child of eleven. In May, 1602, Shakespeare purchased one hundred and seven acres of fertile farmland near Stratford and a few months later bought a cottage and garden across the alley from New Place. About 1611, he seems to have returned permanently to Stratford, for the next year a legal document refers to him as "William Shakespeare of Stratford-upon-Avon . . . gentleman." To achieve the desired appellation of gentleman, William Shakespeare had seen to it that the College of Heralds in 1596 granted his father a coat of arms. In one step he thus became a second-generation gentleman.

Shakespeare's daughter Susanna made a good match in 1607 with Dr. John Hall, a prominent and prosperous Stratford physician. His second daughter, Judith, did not marry until she was thirty-one years old, and then, under somewhat scandalous circumstances, she married Thomas Quiney, a Stratford vintner. On March 25, 1616, Shakespeare made his will, bequeathing his landed property to Susanna, £300 to Judith, certain sums to other relatives, and his second-best bed to his wife, Anne. Much has been made of the second-best bed, but the legacy probably indicates only that Anne liked that particular bed. Shakespeare, following the practice of the time, may have already arranged with Susanna for his wife's care. Finally, on April 23, 1616, the anniversary of his birth, William Shakespeare died, and he was buried on April 25 within the chancel of Trinity Church, as befitted an honored citizen. On August 6, 1623, a few months before the publication of the collected edition of Shakespeare's plays, Anne Shakespeare joined her husband in death.

THE PUBLICATION OF HIS PLAYS

During his lifetime Shakespeare made no effort to publish any of his plays, though eighteen appeared in print in single-play editions known as quartos. Some of these are corrupt versions known as "bad quartos." No quarto, so far as is known, had the author's approval. Plays were not considered "literature" any more than most radio and television scripts today are considered literature. Dramatists sold their plays outright to the theatrical companies and it was usually considered in the company's interest to keep plays from getting into print. To achieve a reputation as a man of letters, Shakespeare wrote his *Sonnets* and his narrative poems, *Venus and Adonis* and *The Rape of Lucrece,* but he probably never dreamed that his plays would establish his reputation as a literary genius. Only Ben Jonson, a man known for his colossal conceit, had the crust to call his plays *Works*, as he did when he published an edition in 1616. But men laughed at Ben Jonson.

After Shakespeare's death, two of his old colleagues in the King's Men, John Heminges and Henry Condell, decided that it would be a good thing to print, in more accurate versions than were then available, the plays already published and eighteen additional plays not previously published in quarto. In 1623 appeared *Mr. William Shakespeares Comedies, Histories, & Tragedies. Published according to the True Originall Copies. London. Printed by Isaac Iaggard and Ed. Blount.* This was the famous First Folio, a work that had the authority of Shakespeare's associates. The only play commonly attributed to Shakespeare that was omitted in the First Folio was *Pericles*. In their preface, "To the great Variety of Readers," Heminges and Condell state that whereas "you were abused with diverse stolen and surreptitious copies, maimed and deformed by the frauds and stealths of injurious impostors that exposed them, even those are now offered to your view cured and perfect of their limbs; and all the rest, absolute in their numbers, as he conceived them." What they used for printer's copy is one of the vexed problems of scholarship, and skilled bibliographers have devoted years of study to the question of the relation of the "copy" for the First Folio to Shakespeare's manuscripts. In some cases it is clear that the editors corrected printed quarto versions of the plays, probably by comparison with playhouse scripts. Whether these scripts were in Shakespeare's autograph is anybody's guess. No manuscript of any play in Shakespeare's handwriting has survived. Indeed, very few play manuscripts from this period by any author are extant. The Tudor and Stuart periods had not yet learned to prize autographs and authors' original manuscripts.

Since the First Folio contains eighteen plays not previously printed, it is the only source for these. For the other eighteen, which had appeared in quarto versions, the First Folio also has the authority of an edition prepared and overseen by Shakespeare's colleagues and professional associates. But since editorial standards in 1623 were far from strict, and Heminges and Condell were actors rather than editors by profession, the texts are sometimes careless. The printing and proofreading of the First Folio also left much to be desired, and some garbled passages have had to be corrected and emended. The "good quarto" texts have to be taken into account in preparing a modern edition.

Because of the great popularity of Shakespeare through the centuries, the First Folio has become a prized book, but it is not a very rare one, for it is estimated that 238 copies are extant. The Folger Shakespeare Library in Washington, D.C., has seventy-nine copies of the First Folio, collected by the founder, Henry Clay Folger, who believed that a collation of as many texts as possible would reveal significant facts about the text of Shakespeare's plays. Dr. Charlton Hinman, using an ingenious machine of his own invention for mechanical collating, has made many discoveries that throw light on Shakespeare's text and on printing practices of the day.

The probability is that the First Folio of 1623 had an edition of between 1,000 and 1,250 copies. It is believed that it sold for £1, which made it an expensive book, for £1 in 1623 was equivalent to something between $40 and $50 in modern purchasing power.

During the seventeenth century, Shakespeare was sufficiently popular to warrant three later editions in folio size, the Second Folio of 1632, the Third Folio of 1663–1664, and the Fourth Folio of 1685. The Third Folio added six other plays ascribed to Shakespeare, but these are apocryphal.

THE SHAKESPEAREAN THEATRE

The theatres in which Shakespeare's plays were performed were vastly different from those we know today. The stage was a platform that jutted out into the area now occupied by the first rows of seats on the main floor, what is called the "orchestra" in America and the "pit" in England. This platform had no curtain to come down at the ends of acts and scenes. And although simple stage properties were available, the Elizabethan theatre lacked both the machinery and the elaborate movable scenery of the modern theatre. In the rear of the platform stage was a curtained area that could be used as an inner room, a tomb, or any such scene that might be required. A balcony above this inner room, and perhaps balconies on the sides of the stage, could represent the upper deck of a ship, the entry to Juliet's room, or a prison window. A trap door in the stage provided an entrance for ghosts and devils from the nether regions, and a similar trap in the canopied structure over the stage, known as the "heavens," made it possible to let down angels on a rope. These primitive stage arrangements help to account for many elements in Elizabethan plays. For example, since there was no curtain, the dramatist frequently felt the necessity of writing into his play action to clear the stage at the ends of acts and scenes. The funeral march at the end of *Hamlet* is not there merely for atmosphere; Shakespeare had to get the corpses off the stage. The lack of scenery also freed the dramatist from undue concern about the exact location of his sets, and the physical relation of his various settings to each other did not have to be worked out with the same precision as in the modern theatre.

Before London had buildings designed exclusively for theatrical entertainment, plays were given in inns and taverns. The characteristic inn of the period had an inner courtyard with rooms opening onto balconies overlooking the yard. Players could set up their temporary stages at one end of the yard and audiences could find seats on the balconies out of the weather. The poorer sort could stand or sit on the cobblestones in the yard, which was open to the sky. The first theatres followed this construction, and throughout the Elizabethan period the large public theatres had a yard in front of the stage open to the weather, with two or three tiers of covered balconies extending around the theatre. This physical structure again influenced the writing of plays. Because a dramatist wanted the actors to be heard, he frequently wrote into his play orations that could be delivered with declamatory effect. He also provided spectacle, buffoonery, and broad jests to keep the riotous groundlings in the yard entertained and quiet.

In another respect the Elizabethan theatre differed greatly from ours. It had no actresses. All women's roles were taken by boys, sometimes recruited from the boys' choirs of the London churches. Some of these youths acted their roles with great skill and the Elizabethans did not seem to be aware of any incongruity. The first actresses on the professional English stage appeared after the Restoration of Charles II, in 1660, when exiled Englishmen brought back from France practices of the French stage.

London in the Elizabethan period, as now, was the center of theatrical interest, though wandering actors from time to time traveled through the country performing in inns, halls, and the houses of the nobility. The first professional playhouse, called simply The Theatre, was erected by James Burbage, father of Shakespeare's colleague Richard Burbage, in 1576 on lands of the old Holywell Priory adjacent to Finsbury Fields, a playground and park area just north of the city walls. It had the advantage of being outside the city's jurisdiction and yet was near enough to be easily accessible. Soon after The Theatre was opened, another playhouse called The Curtain was erected in the same neighborhood. Both of these playhouses had open courtyards and were probably polygonal in shape.

About the time The Curtain opened, Richard Farrant, Master of the Children of the Chapel Royal at Windsor and of St. Paul's, conceived the idea of opening a "private" theatre in the old monastery buildings of the Blackfriars, not far from St. Paul's Cathedral in the heart of the city. This theatre was ostensibly to train the choirboys in plays for presentation at Court, but Farrant managed to present plays to paying audiences and achieved considerable success until aristocratic neighbors complained and had the theatre closed. The first Blackfriars Theatre was significant, however, because it popularized the boy actors in a professional way and it paved the way for a second theatre in the Blackfriars, which Shakespeare's company took over more than thirty years later. By the last years of the sixteenth century, London had at least six professional theatres and still others were erected during the reign of James I.

The Globe Theatre, the playhouse that most people connect with Shakespeare, was erected early in 1599 on the Bankside, the area across the Thames from the city. Its construction had a dramatic beginning, for on the night of December 28, 1598, James Burbage's sons, Cuthbert and Richard, gathered together a crew who tore down the old theatre in Holywell and carted the timbers across the river to a site that they had chosen for a new playhouse. The reason for this clandestine operation was a row with the landowner over the lease to the Holywell property. The site chosen for the Globe was another playground outside of the city's jurisdiction, a region of somewhat unsavory character. Not far away was the Bear Garden, an amphitheatre devoted to the baiting of bears and bulls. This was also the region occupied by many houses of ill fame licensed by the Bishop of Winchester and the source of substantial revenue to him. But it was easily accessible either from London Bridge or by means of the cheap boats operated by the London watermen, and it had the great advantage of being beyond the authority of the Puritanical aldermen of London, who frowned on plays because they lured apprentices from work, filled their heads with improper ideas, and generally exerted a bad influence. The aldermen also complained that the crowds drawn together in the theatre helped to spread the plague.

The Globe was the handsomest theatre up to its time. It was a large building, apparently octagonal in shape, and open like its predecessors to the sky in the center, but capable of seating a large audience in its covered balconies. To erect and operate the Globe, the Burbages organized a syndicate composed of the leading members of the dramatic company, of which Shakespeare was a member. Since it was open to the weather and depended on natural light, plays had to be given in the afternoon. This caused no hardship in the long afternoons of an English summer, but in the winter the weather was a great handicap and discouraged all except the hardiest. For that reason, in 1608 Shakespeare's company was glad to take over the lease of the second Blackfriars Theatre, a substantial, roomy hall reconstructed within the framework of the old monastery building. This theatre was protected from the weather and its stage was artificially lighted by chandeliers of candles. This became the winter playhouse for Shakespeare's company and at once proved so popular that the congestion of traffic created an embarrassing problem. Stringent regulations had to be made for the movement of coaches in the vicinity. Shakespeare's company continued to use the Globe during the summer months. In 1613 a squib fired from a cannon during a performance of *Henry VIII* fell on the thatched roof and the Globe burned to the ground. The next year it was rebuilt.

London had other famous theatres. The Rose, just west of the Globe, was built by Philip Henslowe, a semiliterate denizen of the Bankside, who became one of the most important theatrical owners and producers of the Tudor and Stuart periods. What is more important for historians, he kept a detailed account book, which provides much of our information about theatrical history in his time. Another famous theatre on the Bankside was the Swan, which a Dutch priest, Johannes de Witt, visited in 1596. The crude drawing of the stage which he made was copied by his friend Arend van Buchell; it is one of the important pieces of contemporary evidence for theatrical construction. Among the other theatres, the Fortune, north of the city, on Golding Lane, and the Red Bull, even farther away from the city, off St. John's Street, were the most popular. The Red Bull, much frequented by apprentices, favored sensational and sometimes rowdy plays.

The actors who kept all of these theatres going were organized into companies under the protection of some noble patron. Traditionally actors had enjoyed a low reputation. In some of the ordinances they were classed as vagrants; in the phraseology of the time, "rogues, vagabonds, sturdy beggars, and common players" were all listed together as undesirables. To escape penalties often meted out to these characters, organized groups of actors managed to gain the protection of various personages of high degree. In the later years of Elizabeth's reign, a group flourished under the name of the Queen's Men; another group had the protection of the Lord Admiral and were known as the Lord Admiral's Men. Edward Alleyn, son-in-law of Philip Henslowe, was the leading spirit in the Lord Admiral's Men. Besides the adult companies, troupes of boy actors from time to time also enjoyed considerable popularity. Among these were the Children of Paul's and the Children of the Chapel Royal.

The company with which Shakespeare had a long association had for its first patron Henry Carey, Lord Hunsdon, the Lord Chamberlain, and hence they were known as the Lord Chamberlain's Men. After the accession of James I, they became the King's Men. This company was the great rival of the Lord Admiral's Men, managed by Henslowe and Alleyn.

All was not easy for the players in Shakespeare's time, for the aldermen of London were always eager for an excuse to close up the Blackfriars and any other theatres in their jurisdiction. The theatres outside the jurisdiction of London were not immune from interference, for they might be shut up by order of the Privy Council for meddling in politics or for various other offenses, or they might be closed in time of plague lest they spread infection. During plague times, the actors usually went on tour and played the provinces wherever they could find an audience. Particularly frightening were the plagues of 1592–1594 and 1613 when the theatres closed and the players, like many other Londoners, had to take to the country.

Though players had a low social status, they enjoyed great popularity, and one of the favorite forms of entertainment at Court was the performance of plays. To be commanded to perform at Court conferred great prestige upon a company of players, and printers frequently noted that fact when they published plays. Several of Shakespeare's plays were performed before the sovereign, and Shakespeare himself undoubtedly acted in some of these plays.

REFERENCES FOR FURTHER READING

Many readers will want suggestions for further reading about Shakespeare and his times. A few references will serve as guides to further study in the enormous literature on the subject. A simple and useful little book is Gerald Sanders, *A Shakespeare Primer* (New York, 1950). *A Companion to Shakespeare Studies*, edited by Harley Granville-Barker and G. B. Harrison (Cambridge, 1934), is a valuable guide. The most recent concise handbook of facts about Shakespeare is Gerald E. Bentley, *Shakespeare: A Biographical Handbook* (New Haven, 1961). More detailed but not so voluminous as to be confusing is Hazelton Spencer, *The Art and Life of William Shakespeare* (New York, 1940), which, like Sanders' and Bentley's handbooks, contains a brief annotated list of useful books on various aspects of the subject. The most detailed and scholarly work providing complete factual information about Shakespeare is Sir Edmund Chambers, *William Shakespeare: A Study of Facts and Problems* (2 vols., Oxford, 1930).

Among other biographies of Shakespeare, Joseph Quincy Adams, *A Life of William Shakespeare* (Boston, 1923) is still an excellent assessment of the essential facts and the traditional information, and Marchette Chute, *Shakespeare of London* (New York, 1949; paperback, 1957) stresses Shakespeare's life in the theatre. Two new biographies of Shakespeare have recently appeared. A. L. Rowse, *William Shakespeare: A Biography* (London, 1963; New York, 1964) provides an appraisal by a distinguished English historian, who dismisses the notion that somebody else wrote Shakespeare's plays as arrant nonsense that runs counter to known historical fact. Peter Quennell, *Shakespeare: A Biography* (Cleveland and New York, 1963) is a sensitive and intelligent survey of what is known and surmised of Shakespeare's life. Louis B. Wright, *Shakespeare for Everyman* (New York, 1964; 1965) discusses the basis of Shakespeare's enduring popularity.

The *Shakespeare Quarterly*, published by the Shakespeare Association of America under the editorship of James G. McManaway, is recommended for those who wish to keep up with current Shakespearean scholarship and stage productions. The *Quarterly* includes an annual bibliography of Shakespeare editions and works on Shakespeare published during the previous year.

The question of the authenticity of Shakespeare's

plays arouses perennial attention. The theory of hidden cryptograms in the plays is demolished by William F. and Elizebeth S. Friedman, *The Shakespearean Ciphers Examined* (New York, 1957). A succinct account of the various absurdities advanced to suggest the authorship of a multitude of candidates other than Shakespeare will be found in R. C. Churchill, *Shakespeare and His Betters* (Bloomington, Ind., 1959). Another recent discussion of the subject, *The Authorship of Shakespeare,* by James G. McManaway (Washington, D.C., 1962), presents the evidence from contemporary records to prove the identity of Shakespeare the actor-playwright with Shakespeare of Stratford.

Scholars are not in agreement about the details of playhouse construction in the Elizabethan period. John C. Adams presents a plausible reconstruction of the Globe in *The Globe Playhouse: Its Design and Equipment* (Cambridge, Mass., 1942; 2nd rev. ed., 1961). A description with excellent drawings based on Dr. Adams' model is Irwin Smith, *Shakespeare's Globe Playhouse: A Modern Reconstruction in Text and Scale Drawings* (New York, 1956). Other sensible discussions are C. Walter Hodges, *The Globe Restored* (London, 1953) and A. M. Nagler, *Shakespeare's Stage* (New Haven, 1958). Bernard Beckerman, *Shakespeare at the Globe, 1599–1609* (New Haven, 1962; paperback, 1962) discusses Elizabethan staging and acting techniques.

A sound and readable history of the early theatres is Joseph Quincy Adams, *Shakespearean Playhouses: A History of English Theatres from the Beginnings to the Restoration* (Boston, 1917). For detailed, factual information about the Elizabethan and seventeenth-century stages, the definitive reference works are Sir Edmund Chambers, *The Elizabethan Stage* (4 vols., Oxford, 1923) and Gerald E. Bentley, *The Jacobean and Caroline Stages* (5 vols., Oxford, 1941–1956).

Further information on the history of the theatre and related topics will be found in the following titles: T. W. Baldwin, *The Organization and Personnel of the Shakespearean Company* (Princeton, 1927); Lily Bess Campbell, *Scenes and Machines on the English Stage during the Renaissance* (Cambridge, 1923); Esther Cloudman Dunn, *Shakespeare in America* (New York, 1939); George C. D. Odell, *Shakespeare from Betterton to Irving* (2 vols., London, 1931); Arthur Colby Sprague, *Shakespeare and the Actors: The Stage Business in His Plays (1660–1905)* (Cambridge, Mass., 1944) and *Shakespearian Players and Performances* (Cambridge, Mass., 1953); Leslie Hotson, *The Commonwealth and Restoration Stage* (Cambridge, Mass., 1928); Alwin Thaler, *Shakspere to Sheridan: A Book about the Theatre of Yesterday and To-day* (Cambridge, Mass., 1922); George C. Branam, *Eighteenth-Century Adaptations of Shakespeare's Tragedies* (Berkeley, 1956); C. Beecher Hogan, *Shakespeare in the Theatre, 1701–1800* (Oxford, 1957); Ernest Bradlee Watson, *Sheridan to Robertson: A Study of the 19th-Century London Stage* (Cambridge, Mass., 1926); and Enid Welsford, *The Court Masque* (Cambridge, Mass., 1927).

A brief account of the growth of Shakespeare's reputation is F. E. Halliday, *The Cult of Shakespeare* (London, 1947). A more detailed discussion is given in Augustus Ralli, *A History of Shakespearian Criticism* (2 vols., Oxford, 1932; New York, 1958). Harley Granville-Barker, *Prefaces to Shakespeare* (5 vols., London, 1927–1948; 2 vols., London, 1958) provides stimulating critical discussion of the plays. An older classic of criticism is Andrew C. Bradley, *Shakespearean Tragedy: Lectures on Hamlet, Othello, King Lear, Macbeth* (London, 1904; paperback, 1955). Sir Edmund Chambers, *Shakespeare: A Survey* (London, 1935; paperback, 1958) contains short, sensible essays on thirty-four of the plays, originally written as introductions to single-play editions. Alfred Harbage, *William Shakespeare: A Reader's Guide* (New York, 1963) is a handbook to the reading and appreciation of the plays, with scene synopses and interpretation.

For the history plays see Lily Bess Campbell, *Shakespeare's "Histories": Mirrors of Elizabethan Policy* (Cambridge, 1947); John Palmer, *Political Characters of Shakespeare* (London, 1945; 1961); E. M. W. Tillyard, *Shakespeare's History Plays* (London, 1948); Irving Ribner, *The English History Play in the Age of Shakespeare* (Princeton, 1947); Max M. Reese, *The Cease of Majesty* (London, 1961); and Arthur Colby Sprague, *Shakespeare's Histories: Plays for the Stage* (London, 1964). Harold Jenkins, "Shakespeare's History Plays: 1900–1951," *Shakespeare Survey 6* (Cambridge, 1953),

1–15, provides an excellent survey of recent critical opinion on the subject.

In addition to the titles listed above, a number of other works provide critical and historical background for study of the *Henry VI* plays. Paul M. Kendall, *The Yorkist Age: Daily Life during the Wars of the Roses* (New York, 1962) devotes a chapter to a lucid summary of the course of the conflict between York and Lancaster and describes the various battles. S. B. Chrimes, *Lancastrians, Yorkists, and Henry VII* (London & New York, 1964) presents a full explication of the dynastic problem resulting from Edward III's many children and the course of events leading up to Henry VII's assumption of the throne. C. L. Kingsford, *Prejudice and Promise in Fifteenth Century England* (Oxford, 1925) has a valuable chapter on Shakespeare's treatment of fifteenth-century English history. Hereward T. Price, *Construction in Shakespeare,* University of Michigan Contributions in Modern Philology, No. 17 (Ann Arbor, 1951), argues for a unified pattern to the three parts of *Henry VI* and Shakespeare's sole authorship and defends the skill of their construction. The most recent edition of the trilogy has been edited by Andrew S. Cairncross for the new Arden series (3 vols., London & Cambridge, Mass., 1962–1964).

The comedies are illuminated by the following studies: C. L. Barber, *Shakespeare's Festive Comedy* (Princeton, 1959); John Russell Brown, *Shakespeare and His Comedies* (London, 1957); H. B. Charlton, *Shakespearian Comedy* (London, 1938; 4th ed.,

1949); W. W. Lawrence, *Shakespeare's Problem Comedies* (New York, 1931); and Thomas M. Parrott, *Shakespearean Comedy* (New York, 1949).

Further discussions of Shakespeare's tragedies, in addition to Bradley, already cited, are contained in H. B. Charlton, *Shakespearian Tragedy* (Cambridge, 1948); Willard Farnham, *The Medieval Heritage of Elizabethan Tragedy* (Berkeley, 1936) and *Shakespeare's Tragic Frontier: The World of His Final Tragedies* (Berkeley, 1950); and Harold S. Wilson, *On the Design of Shakespearian Tragedy* (Toronto, 1957).

The "Roman" plays are treated in M. M. MacCallum, *Shakespeare's Roman Plays and Their Background* (London, 1910) and J. C. Maxwell, "Shakespeare's Roman Plays, 1900–1956," *Shakespeare Survey 10* (Cambridge, 1957), 1–11.

Kenneth Muir, *Shakespeare's Sources: Comedies and Tragedies* (London, 1957) discusses Shakespeare's use of source material. The sources themselves have been reprinted several times. Among old editions are John P. Collier (ed.), *Shakespeare's Library* (2 vols., London, 1850), Israel C. Gollancz (ed.), *The Shakespeare Classics* (12 vols., London, 1907–1926), and W. C. Hazlitt (ed.), *Shakespeare's Library* (6 vols., London, 1875). A modern edition is being prepared by Geoffrey Bullough with the title *Narrative and Dramatic Sources of Shakespeare* (London and New York, 1957–). Five volumes, covering the sources for the comedies, histories, and Roman plays, have been published to date (1966).

In addition to the second edition of *Webster's*

New International Dictionary, which contains most of the unusual words used by Shakespeare, the following reference works are helpful: Edwin A. Abbott, *A Shakespearian Grammar* (London, 1872); C. T. Onions, *A Shakespeare Glossary* (2nd rev. ed., Oxford, 1925); and Eric Partridge, *Shakespeare's Bawdy* (New York, 1948; paperback, 1960).

Some knowledge of the social background of the period in which Shakespeare lived is important for a full understanding of his work. A brief, clear, and accurate account of Tudor history is S. T. Bindoff, *The Tudors*, in the Penguin series. A readable general history is G. M. Trevelyan, *The History of England*, first published in 1926 and available in numerous editions. The same author's *English Social History*, first published in 1942 and also available in many editions, provides fascinating information about England in all periods. Sir John Neale, *Queen Elizabeth* (London, 1935; paperback, 1957) is the best study of the great Queen. Various aspects of life in the Elizabethan period are treated in Louis B. Wright, *Middle-Class Culture in Elizabethan England* (Chapel Hill, N.C., 1935; reprinted Ithaca, N.Y., 1958, 1964). *Shakespeare's England: An Account of the Life and Manners of His Age*, edited by Sidney Lee and C. T. Onions (2 vols., Oxford, 1917), provides much information on many aspects of Elizabethan life. A fascinating survey of the period will be found in Muriel St. C. Byrne, *Elizabethan Life in Town and Country* (London, 1925; rev. ed., 1954; paperback, 1961).

The Folger Library is issuing a series of illustrated

booklets entitled "Folger Booklets on Tudor and Stuart Civilization," printed and distributed by Cornell University Press. Published to date are the following titles:

D. W. Davies, *Dutch Influences on English Culture, 1558–1625*
Giles E. Dawson, *The Life of William Shakespeare*
Ellen C. Eyler, *Early English Gardens and Garden Books*
Elaine W. Fowler, *English Sea Power in the Early Tudor Period, 1485–1558*
John R. Hale, *The Art of War and Renaissance England*
William Haller, *Elizabeth I and the Puritans*
Virginia A. LaMar, *English Dress in the Age of Shakespeare*
_____, *Travel and Roads in England*
John L. Lievsay, *The Elizabethan Image of Italy*
James G. McManaway, *The Authorship of Shakespeare*
Dorothy E. Mason, *Music in Elizabethan England*
Garrett Mattingly, *The "Invincible" Armada and Elizabethan England*
Boies Penrose, *Tudor and Early Stuart Voyaging*
T. I. Rae, *Scotland in the Time of Shakespeare*
Conyers Read, *The Government of England under Elizabeth*
Albert J. Schmidt, *The Yeoman in Tudor and Stuart England*
Lilly C. Stone, *English Sports and Recreations*

Craig R. Thompson, *The Bible in English, 1525–1611*

———, *The English Church in the Sixteenth Century*

———, *Schools in Tudor England*

———, *Universities in Tudor England*

Louis B. Wright, *Shakespeare's Theatre and the Dramatic Tradition*

At intervals the Folger Library plans to gather these booklets in hardbound volumes. The first is *Life and Letters in Tudor and Stuart England, First Folger Series,* edited by Louis B. Wright and Virginia A. LaMar (published for the Folger Shakespeare Library by Cornell University Press, 1962). The volume contains eleven of the separate booklets.

Britain during the Wars of the Roses

Actual Chronology for Events in the Three Parts of Henry VI

1421	
Dec. 6	Birth of Henry VI at Windsor.
1422	
Aug. 31	Death of Henry V at Vincennes.
Oct. 21	Charles VI of France dies, succeeded by Charles VII.
Nov. 7	Body of Henry V lies in state in Westminster Abbey.
Nov. 9	Parliament summoned.
1423	
Aug. 1	Salisbury defeats French at Cravant.
1424	
Aug. 17	Bedford defeats French at Verneuil.
1425	
Aug. 2	Salisbury takes Le Mans.
Oct. 1	Gloucester and Winchester clash in London.
1427	
Sept. 5	Dunois, Bastard of Orléans, defeats English at Montargis.
1429	
May 1–3	Joan of Arc raises the siege of Orléans.
July 17	Charles VII crowned at Reims.
Nov. 6	Henry VI crowned at Westminster.
1430	
May 23	Joan of Arc captured at Compiègne.
1431	
May 30	Joan of Arc burned at Rouen.

Dec. 16	Henry VI crowned in Notre Dame, Paris.
1435	
Sept. 15	Death of John, Duke of Bedford.
1436	French recover Paris.
1444	
May 28	Two-year Anglo-French truce signed at Tours.
1445	
April 22	Henry VI marries Margaret of Anjou.
1448	
May	French recover Maine and Anjou by marriage treaty.
1450–54	Jack Cade's Rebellion.
1451	French conquer Guienne.
1453	English retain only Calais and Channel Islands of French possessions.
1454	
March 27	Richard, Duke of York, made Protector.
1455	
May 22	1st Battle of St. Albans; Yorkist victory.
1460	
July 10	Battle of Northampton; Yorkist victory.
Dec. 30	Battle of Wakefield; Lancastrian victory; death of Duke of York.
1461	
Feb. 2	Battle of Mortimer's Cross; Yorkist victory.
Feb. 17	2nd Battle of St. Albans; Lancastrian victory.
March 1	Edward, Earl of March, acclaimed King in London.

March 29	Battle of Towton; rout of Lancastrians.
June 28	Coronation of Edward IV; Henry VI and Margaret of Anjou retire to Scotland.
July 22	Death of Charles VII of France; succeeded by Louis XI.
1469	
July 26	Battle of Banbury; victory of Warwick against forces of Edward IV.
1470	
Oct. 13	Henry VI restored to throne.
1471	
April 14	Battle of Barnet; Yorkist victory; death of Earl of Warwick.
May 4	Battle of Tewkesbury; decisive Yorkist victory; death of Edward, Prince of Wales.

HOUSE OF LANCASTER

JOHN OF GAUNT, DUKE OF LANCASTER

(4th son of EDWARD III)

Legitimate line
(*m.* Blanche of Lancaster)

King Henry IV

King Henry V
(*m.* Catherine Valois)
d. 1422

King Henry VI
(*m.* Margaret of Anjou)
d. 1471

Edward,
Prince of Wales
d. 1471

Thomas,
Duke of Clarence
d. 1421

John,
Duke of Bedford
d. 1435

Humphrey,
Duke of Gloucester
d. 1446

Beaufort line
Catherine Swynford (mistress and at last wife)

John,
1st Earl of Somerset
d. 1410

Henry,
2nd Earl of Somerset
d. 1418

John,
1st Duke of Somerset
d. 1444

Margaret Beaufort
(*m.* Edmund Tudor,
Earl of Richmond)

Henry VII

House of Tudor

Edmund,
2nd Duke of Somerset
d. 1455

Henry,
3rd Duke of Somerset
d. 1464

Edmund
called
4th Duke of Somerset
d. 1471

Jane
d. 1445

House of Stuart

Henry,
Bshp. of Winchester
d. 1447

Thomas,
Duke of Exeter
d. 1426

Joan

House of Neville

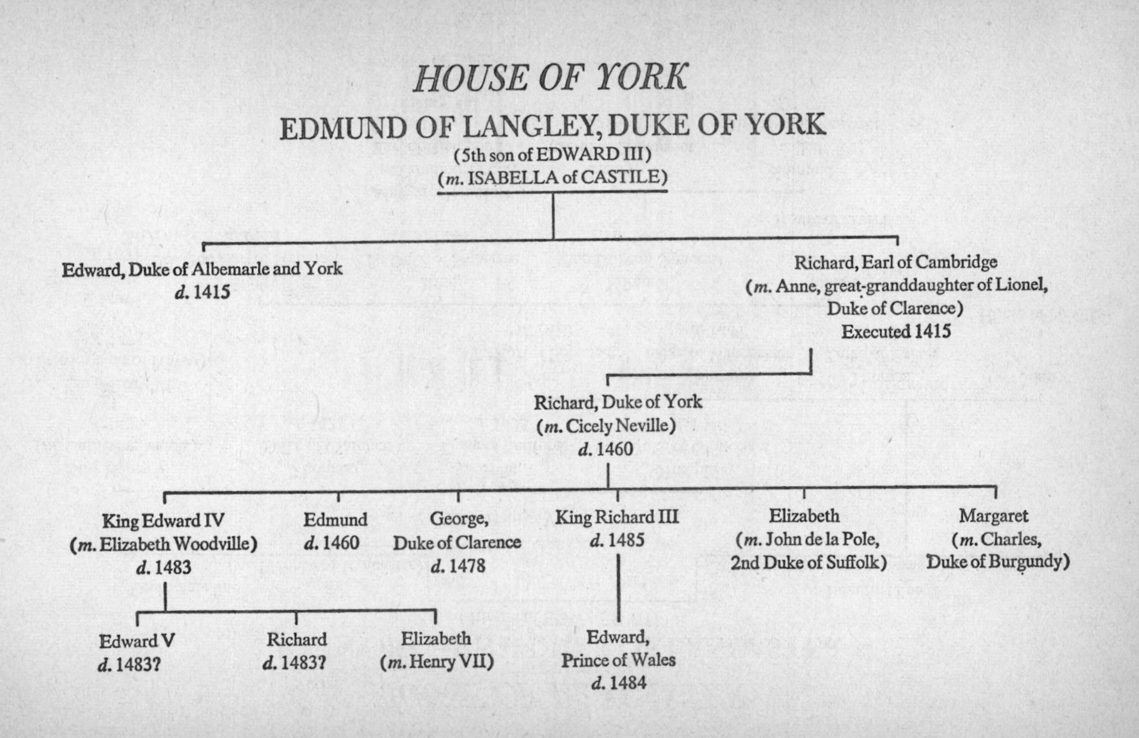
HOUSE OF YORK
EDMUND OF LANGLEY, DUKE OF YORK
(5th son of EDWARD III)
(m. ISABELLA of CASTILE)
Edward, Duke of Albemarle and York
d. 1415
Richard, Earl of Cambridge
(m. Anne, great-granddaughter of Lionel,
Duke of Clarence)
Executed 1415
Richard, Duke of York
(m. Cicely Neville)
d. 1460
King Edward IV
(m. Elizabeth Woodville)
d. 1483
Edmund
d. 1460
George,
Duke of Clarence
d. 1478
King Richard III
d. 1485
Elizabeth
(m. John de la Pole,
2nd Duke of Suffolk)
Margaret
(m. Charles,
Duke of Burgundy)
Edward V
d. 1483?
Richard
d. 1483?
Elizabeth
(m. Henry VII)
Edward,
Prince of Wales
d. 1484

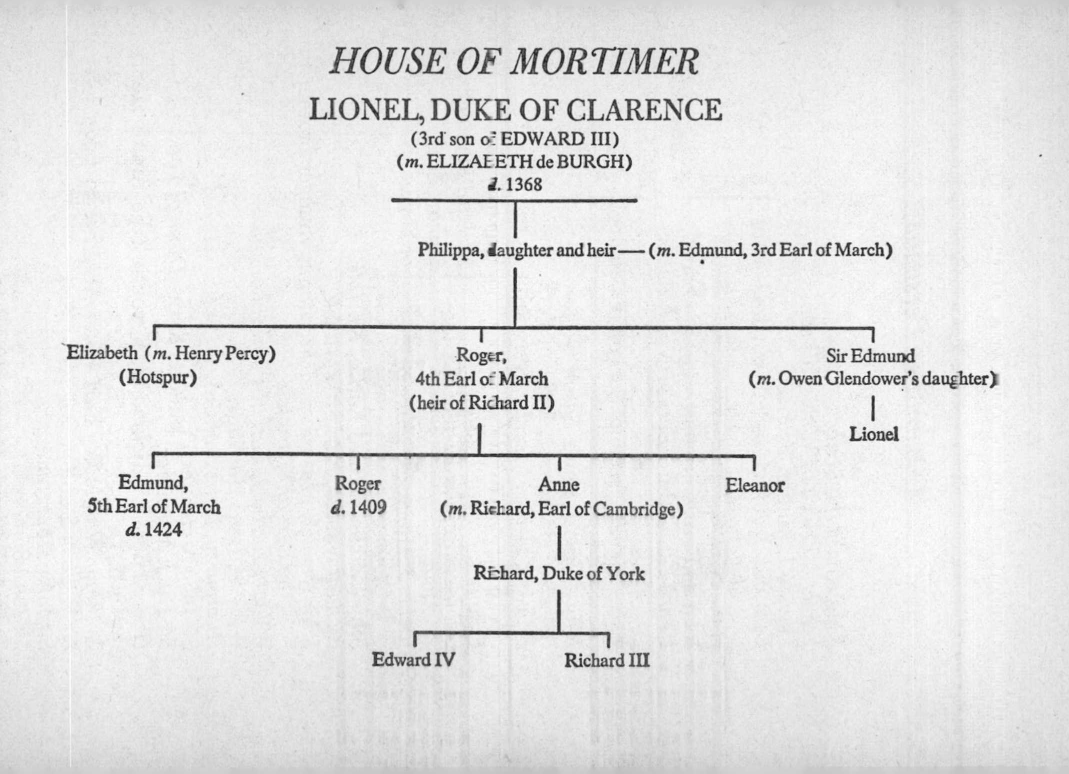
HOUSE OF MORTIMER
LIONEL, DUKE OF CLARENCE
(3rd son of EDWARD III)
(m. ELIZABETH de BURGH)
d. 1368
Philippa, daughter and heir — (m. Edmund, 3rd Earl of March)
Elizabeth (m. Henry Percy)
(Hotspur)
Roger,
4th Earl of March
(heir of Richard II)
Sir Edmund
(m. Owen Glendower's daughter)
Lionel
Edmund,
5th Earl of March
d. 1424
Roger
d. 1409
Anne
(m. Richard, Earl of Cambridge)
Eleanor
Richard, Duke of York
Edward IV
Richard III

[*Dramatis Personae*

King Henry the Sixth.
Edward, Prince of Wales, his son.
Lewis XI, King of France.
Edmund Beaufort, styled fourth *Duke of Somerset,*
Henry Holland, Duke of Exeter,
John de Vere, thirteenth *Earl of Oxford,*
Henry Percy, third *Earl of Northumberland,*
Ralph Neville, second *Earl of Westmorland,*
John Clifford, ninth *Baron Clifford.*
} of the King's party.
Richard Plantagenet, Duke of York.
Edward, Earl of March, afterward *King Edward IV,*
Edmund, Earl of Rutland,
George, afterward *Duke of Clarence,*
Richard, afterward *Duke of Gloucester.*
} sons to *Richard Plantagenet, Duke of York.*
John Mowbray, third *Earl of Norfolk.*
Richard Neville, Earl of Warwick.
John Neville, Marquess of Montagu, younger brother to the *Earl of Warwick.*
William Herbert, Earl of Pembroke.
William, Lord Hastings.
Humphrey, Lord Stafford.
Sir John Mortimer,
Sir Hugh Mortimer,
} uncles to the *Duke of York.*
Henry, Earl of Richmond, a youth (the future Henry VII).
Anthony Woodville, Earl Rivers, brother to *Lady Grey.*
Sir William Stanley.
Sir John Montgomery.
Sir John Somerville.
Tutor to Rutland; Mayor of York.

Lieutenant of the Tower; a Nobleman.
Two Keepers; a Huntsman.
A Son that has killed his Father.
A Father that has killed his Son.

Queen Margaret.
Lady Elizabeth Grey, afterward queen to *Edward IV.*
The Lady Bona, sister to the French queen.
Soldiers, Attendants, Messengers, Watchmen, etc.

SCENE: *England and France.*]

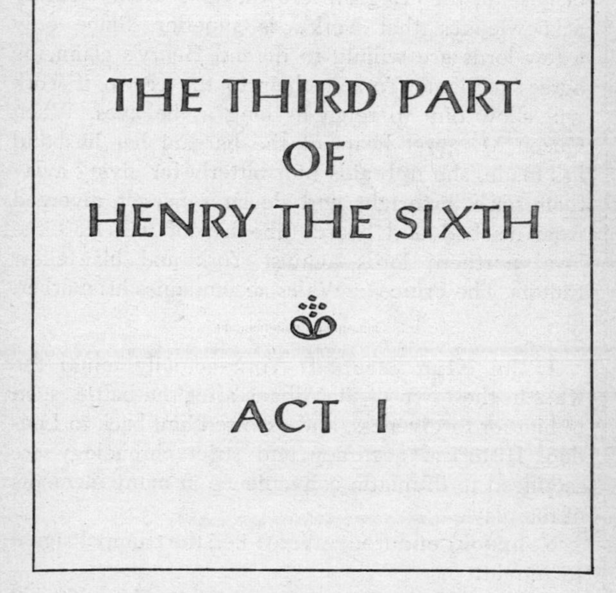

THE THIRD PART OF HENRY THE SIXTH

ACT I

I.i. Having defeated the King's forces, York, with his sons and allies, arrives at London. At Warwick's urging, York seats himself on the throne, where the King finds him when he enters to convene Parliament. York and King Henry argue their respective claims to the English crown, and Henry tacitly acknowledges that York's is superior. Since only a few lords are willing to defend Henry's claim, he agrees to name York as heir to the crown if York will allow him to reign as long as he lives. When Queen Margaret hears of the bargain her husband has made, she upbraids him bitterly for giving away their son's birthright and declares herself divorced from his bed and board. She herself will lead the loyal northern lords against York and his fellow traitors. The Prince of Wales accompanies his mother.

---

1. **the King escaped:** York actually found the King in the town of St. Albans after the battle, sued to him for forgiveness, and escorted him back to London. Historical accuracy and strict chronology are sacrificed to dramatic convenience in many elements of the play.

5. **brook:** endure; **retreat:** i.e., the trumpet signal to retreat.

7. **Lord Clifford:** in *2 Henry VI* the elder Clifford is killed at St. Albans by York. The apparent inconsistency may be the result of compressed phraseology here.

12. **beaver:** the visor of a helmet.

16. **encountered:** engaged with.

ACT I

Scene I. [London. The Parliament House.]

Alarum. Enter the Duke of York, Edward, Richard, Norfolk, Montagu, Warwick, and Soldiers.

War. I wonder how the King escaped our hands.
York. While we pursued the horsemen of the North,
He slyly stole away and left his men:
Whereat the great lord of Northumberland,
Whose warlike ears could never brook retreat, 5
Cheered up the drooping army; and himself,
Lord Clifford, and Lord Stafford, all abreast,
Charged our main battle's front and, breaking in,
Were by the swords of common soldiers slain.
Edw. Lord Stafford's father, Duke of Buckingham, 10
Is either slain or wounded dangerous;
I cleft his beaver with a downright blow:
That this is true, father, behold his blood.
[*Showing his bloody sword.*]
Mon. And, brother, here's the Earl of Wiltshire's blood, 15
Whom I encountered as the battles joined.
Rich. Speak thou for me and tell them what I did.

20. **hap:** fortune.

SD 33. **go up:** mount the steps to the throne.

37–8. **Parliament:** York and his friends have just come from their victory at St. Albans (1455), but the events dramatized in this scene took place at the Parliament of 1460, from which the Queen was absent.

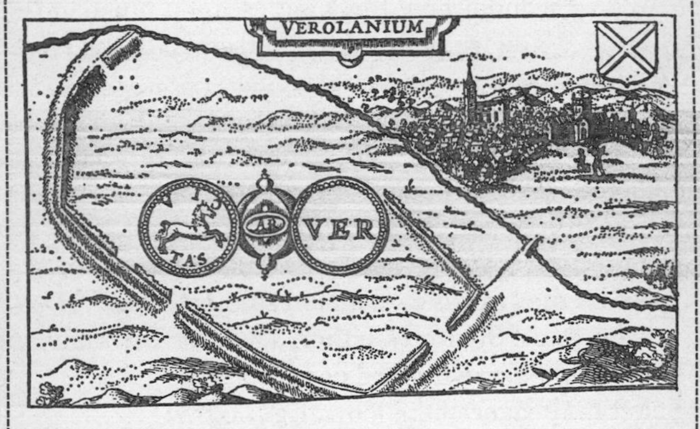

St. Albans. From John Speed, *The Theatre of the Empire of Great Britain* (1627).

[*Throwing down the Duke of Somerset's head.*]

York. Richard hath best deserved of all my sons—
But is your Grace dead, my lord of Somerset?

Nor. Such hap have all the line of John of Gaunt! 20

Rich. Thus do I hope to shake King Henry's head.

War. And so do I. Victorious prince of York,
Before I see thee seated in that throne
Which now the house of Lancaster usurps,
I vow by Heaven these eyes shall never close. 25
This is the palace of the fearful King,
And this the regal seat: possess it, York;
For this is thine and not King Henry's heirs'.

York. Assist me, then, sweet Warwick, and I will;
For hither we have broken in by force. 30

Nor. We'll all assist you: he that flies shall die.

York. Thanks, gentle Norfolk. Stay by me, my lords;
And, soldiers, stay and lodge by me this night.

They go up.

War. And when the King comes, offer him no violence, 35
Unless he seek to thrust you out perforce.

York. The Queen this day here holds her Parliament
But little thinks we shall be of her council.
By words or blows here let us win our right. 40

Rich. Armed as we are, let's stay within this house.

War. The Bloody Parliament shall this be called,
Unless Plantagenet, Duke of York, be King
And bashful Henry deposed, whose cowardice
Hath made us bywords to our enemies. 45

York. Then leave me not, my lords: be resolute.

49. **holds up:** supports; **Lancaster:** i.e., the King.

50. **bells:** referring to the bells that were attached to the foot of a tame falcon.

51. **plant Plantagenet:** Warwick puns on the fact that this nickname for the Angevin kings derives from the Latin *planta genista* (sprig of broom). York adopted the name **Plantagenet** before Henry VI granted him the family titles and estates.

53. **sturdy:** incorrigible; obstinate.

54. **belike:** perhaps; or, very likely.

57. **father:** killed at St. Albans.

64. **suffer:** allow.

I mean to take possession of my right.
War. Neither the King, nor he that loves him best,
The proudest he that holds up Lancaster,
Dares stir a wing if Warwick shake his bells. 50
I'll plant Plantagenet, root him up who dares.
Resolve thee, Richard: claim the English crown.

Flourish. Enter King Henry, Clifford, Northumberland, Westmorland, Exeter, and the rest.

King H. My lords, look where the sturdy rebel sits,
Even in the chair of state: belike he means,
Backed by the power of Warwick, that false peer, 55
To aspire unto the crown and reign as King.
Earl of Northumberland, he slew thy father,
And thine, Lord Clifford; and you both have vowed revenge
On him, his sons, his favorites, and his friends. 60
North. If I be not, Heavens be revenged on me!
Cliff. The hope thereof makes Clifford mourn in steel.
West. What, shall we suffer this? Let's pluck him down. 65
My heart for anger burns: I cannot brook it.
King H. Be patient, gentle Earl of Westmorland.
Cliff. Patience is for poltroons, such as he:
He durst not sit there had your father lived.
My gracious lord, here in the Parliament 70
Let us assail the family of York.
North. Well hast thou spoken, cousin: be it so.
King H. Ah, know you not the city favors them,

87. **earldom:** the earldom of March, the title by which he claimed the throne as a descendant of Anne Mortimer.

88. **father:** the Earl of Cambridge, executed for a plot on the life of Henry V just before the King sailed for France in 1415.

99. **maintain:** defend.

102. **colors:** battle flags.

From John Speed, *The Theatre of the Empire of Great Britain* (1627).

And they have troops of soldiers at their back?
Exe. But when the Duke is slain, they'll quickly fly. 75
King H. Far be the thought of this from Henry's heart,
To make a shambles of the Parliament House!
Cousin of Exeter, frowns, words, and threats
Shall be the war that Henry means to use. 80
Thou factious Duke of York, descend my throne
And kneel for grace and mercy at my feet:
I am thy sovereign.
York. I am thine.
Exe. For shame, come down: he made thee Duke of York. 85
York. It was my inheritance, as the earldom was.
Exe. Thy father was a traitor to the crown.
War. Exeter, thou art a traitor to the crown
In following this usurping Henry. 90
Cliff. Whom should he follow but his natural king?
War. True, Clifford; and that's Richard Duke of York.
King H. And shall I stand and thou sit in my throne?
95
York. It must and shall be so: content thyself.
War. Be Duke of Lancaster: let him be King.
West. He is both King and Duke of Lancaster;
And that the Lord of Westmorland shall maintain.
War. And Warwick shall disprove it. You forget 100
That we are those which chased you from the field,
And slew your fathers, and with colors spread
Marched through the city to the palace gates.
North. Yes, Warwick, I remember it to my grief;

105. **his:** i.e., that of his father.

117. **father . . . Duke of York:** this is inaccurate; the title Duke of York was held by Cambridge's older brother, Edward, who was killed at the Battle of Agincourt, after Cambridge was already dead.

120. **stoop:** submit themselves.

122. **sith:** since.

123. **Lord Protector:** referring to Humphrey, Duke of Gloucester.

124. **crowned . . . nine months:** Henry was nine months old when he was proclaimed King, but he was not crowned until he was seven.

131. **caviling:** quarreling.

Henry V. From a manuscript commonplace book by Thomas Trevelyan (*ca.* 1608).

And, by his soul, thou and thy house shall rue it. 105
West. Plantagenet, of thee and these thy sons,
Thy kinsmen and thy friends, I'll have more lives
Than drops of blood were in my father's veins.
Cliff. Urge it no more; lest that, instead of words,
I send thee, Warwick, such a messenger 110
As shall revenge his death before I stir.
War. Poor Clifford! how I scorn his worthless threats!
York. Will you we show our title to the crown?
If not, our swords shall plead it in the field. 115
King H. What title hast thou, traitor, to the crown?
Thy father was, as thou art, Duke of York;
Thy grandfather, Roger Mortimer, Earl of March.
I am the son of Henry the Fifth,
Who made the Dauphin and the French to stoop 120
And seized upon their towns and provinces.
War. Talk not of France, sith thou hast lost it all.
King H. The Lord Protector lost it, and not I:
When I was crowned I was but nine months old.
Rich. You are old enough now, and yet, methinks, you lose. 125
Father, tear the crown from the usurper's head.
Edw. Sweet father, do so: set it on your head.
Mon. Good brother, as thou lovest and honorest arms, 130
Let's fight it out and not stand caviling thus.
Rich. Sound drums and trumpets and the King will fly.
York. Sons, peace!

146. **faint:** falter; look uncertain.

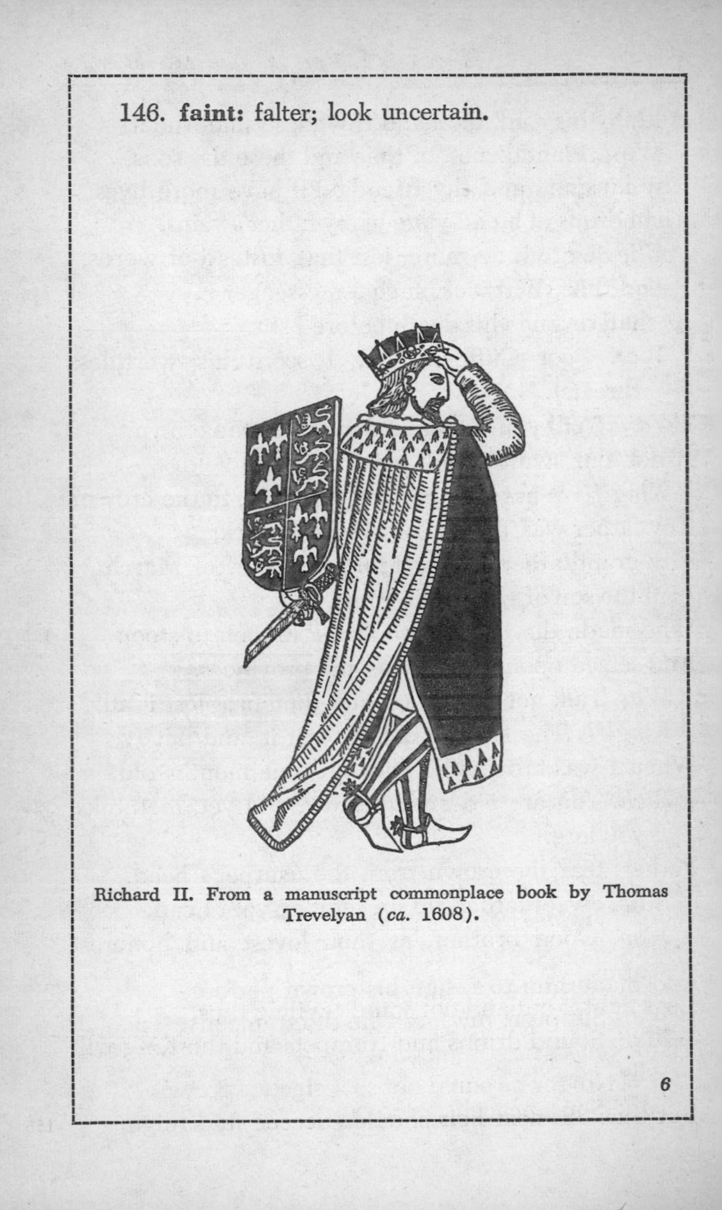

Richard II. From a manuscript commonplace book by Thomas Trevelyan (*ca.* 1608).

King H. Peace, thou! and give King Henry leave to speak. 135
War. Plantagenet shall speak first: hear him, lords;
And be you silent and attentive too,
For he that interrupts him shall not live.
King H. Thinkst thou that I will leave my kingly throne, 140
Wherein my grandsire and my father sat?
No: first shall war unpeople this my realm;
Ay, and their colors, often borne in France,
And now in England to our heart's great sorrow, 145
Shall be my winding sheet. Why faint you, lords?
My title's good, and better far than his.
War. Prove it, Henry, and thou shalt be King.
King H. Henry the Fourth by conquest got the crown. 150
York. 'Twas by rebellion against his king.
King H. [*Aside*] I know not what to say: my title's weak.—
Tell me, may not a king adopt an heir?
York. What then? 155
King H. And if he may, then am I lawful King;
For Richard, in the view of many lords,
Resigned the crown to Henry the Fourth,
Whose heir my father was, and I am his.
York. He rose against him, being his sovereign, 160
And made him to resign his crown perforce.
War. Suppose, my lords, he did it unconstrained,
Think you 'twere prejudicial to his crown?
Exe. No, for he could not so resign his crown
But that the next heir should succeed and reign. 165

190. **usurping blood:** blood of the usurper, King Henry.

King H. Art thou against us, Duke of Exeter?
Exe. His is the right, and therefore pardon me.
York. Why whisper you, my lords, and answer not?
Exe. My conscience tells me he is lawful King.
King H. [*Aside*] All will revolt from me and turn to him. 170
North. Plantagenet, for all the claim thou layst,
Think not that Henry shall be so deposed.
War. Deposed he shall be, in despite of all.
North. Thou art deceived: 'tis not thy southern power 175
Of Essex, Norfolk, Suffolk, nor of Kent,
Which makes thee thus presumptuous and proud,
Can set the Duke up in despite of me.
Cliff. King Henry, be thy title right or wrong, 180
Lord Clifford vows to fight in thy defense.
May that ground gape and swallow me alive
Where I shall kneel to him that slew my father!
King H. O Clifford, how thy words revive my heart!
York. Henry of Lancaster, resign thy crown.— 185
What mutter you, or what conspire you, lords?
War. Do right unto this princely Duke of York,
Or I will fill the house with armed men
And over the chair of state, where now he sits,
Write up his title with usurping blood. 190
He stamps with his foot, and the Soldiers show themselves.
King H. My lord of Warwick, hear but one word:
Let me for this my lifetime reign as King.
York. Confirm the crown to me and to mine heirs,
And thou shalt reign in quiet while thou livest.

207. **bands:** bonds; imprisonment.

216–17. **entail . . . to:** settle upon, as by an entail.

Edward, Prince of Wales. Engraving by Silvester Harding after a drawing in the British Museum.

King H. I am content: Richard Plantagenet, 195
Enjoy the kingdom after my decease.

Cliff. What wrong is this unto the Prince your son!

War. What good is this to England and himself!

West. Base, fearful, and despairing Henry!

Cliff. How hast thou injured both thyself and us! 200

West. I cannot stay to hear these articles.

North. Nor I.

Cliff. Come, cousin, let us tell the Queen these news.

West. Farewell, faint-hearted and degenerate king,
In whose cold blood no spark of honor bides. 205

North. Be thou a prey unto the house of York
And die in bands for this unmanly deed!

Cliff. In dreadful war mayst thou be overcome,
Or live in peace abandoned and despised!
[*Exeunt Northumberland, Clifford, and Westmorland.*]

War. Turn this way, Henry, and regard them not. 210

Exe. They seek revenge and therefore will not yield.

King H. Ah, Exeter!

War. Why should you sigh, my lord?

King H. Not for myself, Lord Warwick, but my son,
Whom I unnaturally shall disinherit. 215
But be it as it may: I here entail
The crown to thee and to thine heirs forever;
Conditionally that here thou take an oath
To cease this civil war and, whilst I live,
To honor me as thy king and sovereign, 220
And neither by treason nor hostility
To seek to put me down and reign thyself.

York. This oath I willingly take and will perform.

226. **forward:** precocious; promising. The King speaks truer than he knows, since Edward, York's eldest son, was thirteen years of age at the time of St. Albans, and Richard was ten years younger. Historically, they would have been eight and eighteen at the time of this scene.

231. **keep:** guard.

233. **unto the sea:** the author seems to have changed his mind about the identity of this character. The statement would fit Thomas Neville, bastard son of William Neville, Lord Falconbridge, who is mentioned in line 267, but Warwick's brother, John Neville, Marquess Montagu, had no sea command. It is possible that Falconbridge originally appeared in this scene instead of Montagu.

235. **bewray:** betray.

240. **gentle:** courteous. The King vainly hopes that she will be **gentle** in the sense "mild" in her reaction to his deed.

241. **extremes:** extremities; dire straits.

War. Long live King Henry! Plantagenet, embrace him. 225

King H. And long live thou and these thy forward sons!

York. Now York and Lancaster are reconciled.

Exe. Accursed be he that seeks to make them foes!

Sennet. Here they come down.

York. Farewell, my gracious lord. I'll to my castle. 230

War. And I'll keep London with my soldiers.

Nor. And I to Norfolk with my followers.

Mont. And I unto the sea from whence I came.

[*Exeunt York and his Sons, Warwick, Norfolk, Montagu, their Soldiers, and Attendants.*]

King H. And I, with grief and sorrow, to the court.

Enter Queen [*Margaret and the Prince of Wales*].

Exe. Here comes the Queen, whose looks bewray her anger: 235
I'll steal away.

King H. Exeter, so will I.

Queen M. Nay, go not from me: I will follow thee.

King H. Be patient, gentle queen, and I will stay. 240

Queen M. Who can be patient in such extremes?
Ah, wretched man! would I had died a maid
And never seen thee, never borne thee son,
Seeing thou hast proved so unnatural a father!
Hath he deserved to lose his birthright thus? 245
Hadst thou but loved him half so well as I,
Or felt that pain which I did for him once,
Or nourished him as I did with my blood,

261. **head:** advantage.

262. **sufferance:** permission.

266. **Warwick is Chancellor:** another puzzling error. After the victory at St. Albans, when York reorganized the government, he appointed Warwick Captain of Calais but not Chancellor. Warwick's father, the Earl of Salisbury, had been appointed Chancellor in 1454, but at the time of York's reorganization, the chancellorship was held by Thomas Bourchier, Archbishop of Canterbury. The line may have originally designated Salisbury as Chancellor. Salisbury does not appear in this play; he died after the Battle of Wakefield in 1460.

267. **Narrow Seas:** English Channel.

271. **silly:** feeble; defenseless.

273. **granted:** acceded.

Thou wouldst have left thy dearest heartblood there,
Rather than have made that savage Duke thine heir 250
And disinherited thine only son.

Prince. Father, you cannot disinherit me:
If you be King, why should not I succeed?

King H. Pardon me, Margaret. Pardon me, sweet son. 255
The Earl of Warwick and the Duke enforced me.

Queen M. Enforced thee! Art thou King, and wilt be forced?
I shame to hear thee speak. Ah, timorous wretch!
Thou hast undone thyself, thy son, and me; 260
And giv'n unto the house of York such head
As thou shalt reign but by their sufferance.
To entail him and his heirs unto the crown,
What is it but to make thy sepulcher,
And creep into it far before thy time? 265
Warwick is Chancellor and the lord of Calais;
Stern Falconbridge commands the Narrow Seas;
The Duke is made Protector of the realm:
And yet shalt thou be safe? Such safety finds
The trembling lamb environed with wolves. 270
Had I been there, which am a silly woman,
The soldiers should have tossed me on their pikes
Before I would have granted to that act.
But thou preferrst thy life before thine honor:
And, seeing thou dost, I here divorce myself 275
Both from thy table, Henry, and thy bed,
Until that act of Parliament be repealed
Whereby my son is disinherited.
The northern lords that have forsworn thy colors

299. **coast:** attack.

300. **Tire:** prey.

302. **entreat them fair:** treat them graciously, in a conciliatory manner.

Will follow mine, if once they see them spread; 280
And spread they shall be, to thy foul disgrace
And utter ruin of the house of York.
Thus do I leave thee. Come, son, let's away:
Our army is ready. Come, we'll after them.

King H. Stay, gentle Margaret, and hear me speak. 285

Queen M. Thou hast spoke too much already: get thee gone.

King H. Gentle son Edward, thou wilt stay with me?

Queen M. Ay, to be murdered by his enemies. 290

Prince. When I return with victory from the field
I'll see your Grace: till then I'll follow her.

Queen M. Come, son, away: we may not linger thus.

[*Exeunt Queen Margaret and the Prince of Wales.*]

King H. Poor queen! how love to me and to her son 295
Hath made her break out into terms of rage!
Revenged may she be on that hateful duke,
Whose haughty spirit, winged with desire,
Will coast my crown and, like an empty eagle,
Tire on the flesh of me and of my son! 300
The loss of those three lords torments my heart:
I'll write unto them and entreat them fair.
Come, cousin, you shall be the messenger.

Exe. And I, I hope, shall reconcile them all.

Exeunt.

I.[ii.] At York's stronghold in Yorkshire, his sons and Warwick's brother persuade him to break his oath and claim the crown. No sooner is the decision made than a message announces that the Queen with 20,000 men is about to besiege the castle. Though his own forces are no more than 5,000 strong, York and his sons prepare to meet the Lancastrians in battle.

4. **brother:** perhaps another indication that this character was originally named Falconbridge; the elder Falconbridge was York's brother-in-law.

14. **breathe:** rest.

19–20. **forsworn:** perjured.

[Scene II. Sandal Castle.]

Flourish. Enter Richard, Edward, and Montagu.

Rich. Brother, though I be youngest, give me leave.
Edw. No, I can better play the orator.
Mon. But I have reasons strong and forcible.

Enter the Duke of York.

York. Why, how now, sons and brother! At a strife?
What is your quarrel? How began it first? 5
Edw. No quarrel, but a slight contention.
York. About what?
Rich. About that which concerns your Grace and us:
The crown of England, father, which is yours. 10
York. Mine, boy? Not until King Henry be dead.
Rich. Your right depends not on his life or death.
Edw. Now you are heir, therefore enjoy it now.
By giving the house of Lancaster leave to breathe,
It will outrun you, father, in the end. 15
York. I took an oath that he should quietly reign.
Edw. But for a kingdom any oath may be broken:
I would break a thousand oaths to reign one year.
Rich. No: God forbid your Grace should be forsworn. 20
York. I shall be, if I claim by open war.

28. **depose:** testify on oath.

29. **frivolous:** without weight.

33. **feign:** invent; fable.

38. **presently:** at once.

41. **privily:** confidentially; privately.

42. **Lord Cobham:** Edward Brooke, Lord Cobham, of Kent.

45. **Witty:** intelligent; **liberal:** gentlemanly.

46. **what resteth more:** what else needs to be done.

47. **rise:** rebel.

48. **And yet the King not privy to my drift:** without the King being aware of my intention.

Rich. I'll prove the contrary, if you'll hear me speak.
York. Thou canst not, son; it is impossible.
Rich. An oath is of no moment, being not took
Before a true and lawful magistrate 25
That hath authority over him that swears.
Henry had none but did usurp the place;
Then, seeing 'twas he that made you to depose,
Your oath, my lord, is vain and frivolous.
Therefore, to arms! And, father, do but think 30
How sweet a thing it is to wear a crown,
Within whose circuit is Elysium
And all that poets feign of bliss and joy.
Why do we linger thus? I cannot rest
Until the white rose that I wear be dyed 35
Even in the lukewarm blood of Henry's heart.
York. Richard, enough: I will be King or die.
Brother, thou shalt to London presently
And whet on Warwick to this enterprise.
Thou, Richard, shalt to the Duke of Norfolk 40
And tell him privily of our intent.
You, Edward, shall unto my Lord Cobham,
With whom the Kentishmen will willingly rise:
In them I trust; for they are soldiers,
Witty, courteous, liberal, full of spirit. 45
While you are thus employed, what resteth more
But that I seek occasion how to rise,
And yet the King not privy to my drift,
Nor any of the house of Lancaster?

Enter [a Messenger].

50. **post:** haste.
54. **hard:** near.
59. **post:** ride posthaste.
62. **policy:** craft.
66. **Sir John and Sir Hugh:** apparently bastards of the family of York's mother.
67. **happy:** fortunate.
72. **for a need:** if need be.
75. **straight:** immediately.

But, stay! What news? Why comest thou in such post? 50
Mess. The Queen, with all the northern earls and lords,
Intend here to besiege you in your castle.
She is hard by with twenty thousand men;
And therefore fortify your hold, my lord. 55
York. Ay, with my sword. What! thinkst thou that we fear them?
Edward and Richard, you shall stay with me.
My brother Montagu shall post to London.
Let noble Warwick, Cobham, and the rest, 60
Whom we have left protectors of the King,
With pow'rful policy strengthen themselves
And trust not simple Henry nor his oaths.
Mon. Brother, I go: I'll win them, fear it not.
And thus most humbly I do take my leave. *Exit.* 65

Enter [Sir John] Mortimer and his brother [Sir Hugh Mortimer].

York. Sir John and Sir Hugh Mortimer, mine uncles,
You are come to Sandal in a happy hour:
The army of the Queen mean to besiege us.
Sir John. She shall not need: we'll meet her in the field. 70
York. What, with five thousand men?
Rich. Ay, with five hundred, father, for a need.
A woman's general: what should we fear?

A march afar off.

Edw. I hear their drums: let's set our men in order
And issue forth and bid them battle straight. 75

80. **Whenas:** when.

I.[**iii.**] York's young son, Edmund, Earl of Rutland, is slain by Young Clifford. Still thirsting to revenge his father's death, Clifford then goes off to seek York himself.

---

12. **pent-up:** an image probably derived from a scene at the Tower menagerie, where lions were frequently kept.

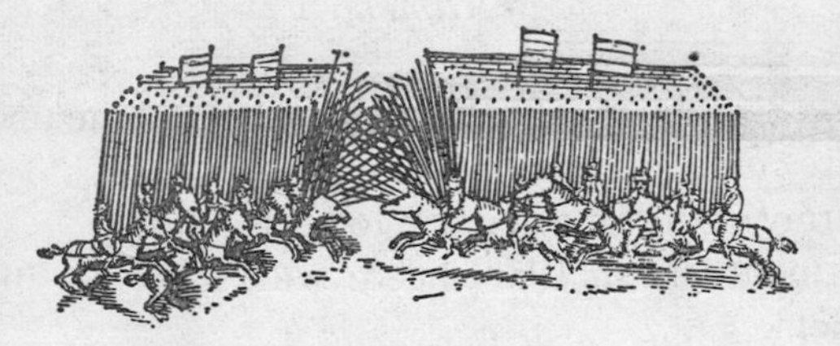

From John Speed, ***The Theatre of the Empire of Great Britain*** **(1627).**

York. Five men to twenty! Though the odds be great,
I doubt not, uncle, of our victory.
Many a battle have I won in France,
Whenas the enemy hath been ten to one. 80
Why should I not now have the like success?

Alarum. Exeunt.

[Scene III. A field of battle betwixt Sandal Castle and Wakefield.]

[*Alarums.*] *Enter Rutland and his Tutor.*

Rut. Ah, whither shall I fly to 'scape their hands?
Ah, tutor, look where bloody Clifford comes!

Enter Clifford [*and Soldiers*].

Cliff. Chaplain, away! Thy priesthood saves thy life.
As for the brat of this accursed duke,
Whose father slew my father, he shall die. 5
Tut. And I, my lord, will bear him company.
Cliff. Soldiers, away with him!
Tut. Ah, Clifford, murder not this innocent child,
Lest thou be hated both of God and man!

Exit, [*dragged off by Soldiers*].

Cliff. How now! is he dead already? or is it fear 10
That makes him close his eyes? I'll open them.
Rut. So looks the pent-up lion o'er the wretch

14. **insulting:** triumphing; exulting.

16. **gentle:** here, as elsewhere in this play, **gentle** refers to birth and implies courteous behavior.

19. **mean:** base; unworthy.

20. **men:** Rutland is supposedly a small child; actually he was only a year younger than Edward.

26. **cope:** encounter; match yourself.

39. **rapier:** sword.

42. **ere I was born:** it is not clear how old the author conceived Rutland as being, but his dialogue does not sound like a child under five years of age; the Battle of Wakefield was five years after Clifford's death at St. Albans.

That trembles under his devouring paws;
And so he walks, insulting o'er his prey,
And so he comes, to rend his limbs asunder. 15
Ah, gentle Clifford, kill me with thy sword
And not with such a cruel threat'ning look.
Sweet Clifford, hear me speak before I die.
I am too mean a subject for thy wrath:
Be thou revenged on men and let me live. 20

Cliff. In vain thou speakst, poor boy: my father's blood
Hath stopped the passage where thy words should enter.

Rut. Then let my father's blood open it again. 25
He is a man, and, Clifford, cope with him.

Cliff. Had I thy brethren here, their lives and thine
Were not revenge sufficient for me;
No, if I digged up thy forefathers' graves
And hung their rotten coffins up in chains, 30
It could not slake mine ire, nor ease my heart.
The sight of any of the house of York
Is as a fury to torment my soul;
And till I root out their accursed line
And leave not one alive, I live in hell. 35
Therefore— [*Lifting his hand.*]

Rut. Oh, let me pray before I take my death!
To thee I pray: sweet Clifford, pity me!

Cliff. Such pity as my rapier's point affords.

Rut. I never did thee harm: why wilt thou slay me? 40

Cliff. Thy father hath.

Rut. But 'twas ere I was born.

51. **Dii faciant laudis summa sit ista tuae:** may the gods make this your most praiseworthy deed (from Ovid, *Heroides*).

53. **cleaving:** clinging.

I. [iv.] York's followers are routed, and York himself is captured by the Queen and her men. Margaret orders York crowned with a paper crown and taunts him with the death of Rutland; she gives him a bloody handkerchief stained with the boy's blood with which to dry his tears. At last, the Queen and Clifford stab York to death. Margaret orders his head cut off and placed on the gates of the city of York.

---

3. **eager:** fierce.

7. **demeaned:** behaved.

9. **make a lane:** mow down the men who barred the way.

Thou hast one son; for his sake pity me,
Lest in revenge thereof, sith God is just,
He be as miserably slain as I. 45
Ah, let me live in prison all my days;
And when I give occasion of offense,
Then let me die, for now thou hast no cause.
Cliff. No cause!
Thy father slew my father: therefore, die. [*Stabs him.*] 50
Rut. Dii faciant laudis summa sit ista tuae! [*Dies.*]
Cliff. Plantagenet! I come, Plantagenet!
And this thy son's blood, cleaving to my blade,
Shall rust upon my weapon till thy blood,
Congealed with this, do make me wipe off both. 55
Exit.

[Scene IV. Another part of the field.]

Alarum. Enter Richard, Duke of York.

York. The army of the Queen hath got the field;
My uncles both are slain in rescuing me;
And all my followers to the eager foe
Turn back and fly, like ships before the wind
Or lambs pursued by hunger-starved wolves. 5
My sons, God knows what hath bechanced them:
But this I know, they have demeaned themselves
Like men born to renown by life or death.
Three times did Richard make a lane to me,
And thrice cried, "Courage, father! fight it out!" 10

12. **purple:** i.e., red; **falchion:** sword.

19. **bodged:** budged; gave way.

20. **bootless:** useless.

29. **butt:** target.

33. **Phaëthon:** son of Phoebus, the sun-god, a symbol of presumptuous folly. When allowed to drive the sun chariot, Phaëthon could not control the horses and had to be slain by Jupiter before he burned up the earth.

34. **noontide prick:** dot of noon.

35. **phoenix:** a legendary bird that existed in only one specimen, which consumed itself on a funeral pyre from which another phoenix then arose.

Phaëthon driving the sun's chariot. From Geoffrey Whitney, *A Choice of Emblems* (1586).

And full as oft came Edward to my side,
With purple falchion, painted to the hilt
In blood of those that had encountered him:
And when the hardiest warriors did retire,
Richard cried, "Charge! and give no foot of ground!" 15
And cried, "A crown, or else a glorious tomb!
A scepter, or an earthly sepulcher!"
With this, we charged again: but, out, alas!
We bodged again; as I have seen a swan
With bootless labor swim against the tide 20
And spend her strength with overmatching waves.
A short alarum within.
Ah, hark! the fatal followers do pursue;
And I am faint and cannot fly their fury;
And were I strong, I would not shun their fury.
The sands are numbered that makes up my life: 25
Here must I stay, and here my life must end.

Enter Queen [Margaret], Clifford, Northumberland, the young Prince and Soldiers.

Come, bloody Clifford, rough Northumberland,
I dare your quenchless fury to more rage:
I am your butt, and I abide your shot.
North. Yield to our mercy, proud Plantagenet. 30
Cliff. Ay, to such mercy as his ruthless arm,
With downright payment, showed unto my father.
Now Phaëthon hath tumbled from his car
And made an evening at the noontide prick.
York. My ashes, as the phoenix, may bring forth 35
A bird that will revenge upon you all:

50. **buckler:** grapple.

57. **grin:** bare his teeth.

59. **spurn:** kick.

61. **ten to one is no impeach of valor:** i.e., the fact that we outnumber him and take advantage of it does not disgrace our valor.

62. **gin:** snare; trap.

66. **true:** honest.

And in that hope I throw mine eyes to Heaven,
Scorning whate'er you can afflict me with.
Why come you not? What! multitudes, and fear?
Cliff. So cowards fight when they can fly no further; 40
So doves do peck the falcon's piercing talons;
So desperate thieves, all hopeless of their lives,
Breathe out invectives 'gainst the officers.
York. O Clifford, but bethink thee once again,
And in thy thought o'errun my former time; 45
And, if thou canst for blushing, view this face
And bite thy tongue, that slanders him with cowardice
Whose frown hath made thee faint and fly ere this!
Cliff. I will not bandy with thee word for word
But buckler with thee blows, twice two for one. 50
Queen M. Hold, valiant Clifford! for a thousand causes
I would prolong awhile the traitor's life.—
Wrath makes him deaf. Speak thou, Northumberland.
North. Hold, Clifford! do not honor him so much 55
To prick thy finger, though to wound his heart.
What valor were it, when a cur doth grin,
For one to thrust his hand between his teeth,
When he might spurn him with his foot away?
It is war's prize to take all vantages; 60
And ten to one is no impeach of valor.
[*They lay hands on York, who struggles.*]
Cliff. Ay, ay, so strives the woodcock with the gin.
North. So doth the cony struggle in the net.
York. So triumph thieves upon their conquered booty; 65
So true men yield, with robbers so o'ermatched.

72. **raught:** reached.

77. **mess:** quartet (from the term for the groups, usually consisting of four persons each, into which banquets were divided).

79. **prodigy:** monster; freak.

81. **wont:** accustomed.

83. **napkin:** handkerchief.

North. What would your Grace have done unto him now?

Queen M. Brave warriors, Clifford and Northumberland, 70
Come, make him stand upon this molehill here,
That raught at mountains with outstretched arms
Yet parted but the shadow with his hand.
What! was it you that would be England's king?
Was't you that reveled in our Parliament 75
And made a preachment of your high descent?
Where are your mess of sons to back you now?
The wanton Edward and the lusty George?
And where's that valiant crookback prodigy,
Dicky your boy, that with his grumbling voice 80
Was wont to cheer his dad in mutinies?
Or, with the rest, where is your darling Rutland?
Look, York: I stained this napkin with the blood
That valiant Clifford, with his rapier's point,
Made issue from the bosom of the boy; 85
And if thine eyes can water for his death,
I give thee this to dry thy cheeks withal.
Alas, poor York! but that I hate thee deadly,
I should lament thy miserable state.
I prithee, grieve, to make me merry, York. 90
What, hath thy fiery heart so parched thine entrails
That not a tear can fall for Rutland's death?
Why art thou patient, man? Thou shouldst be mad;
And I, to make thee mad, do mock thee thus.
Stamp, rave, and fret, that I may sing and dance. 95
Thou wouldst be fee'd, I see, to make me sport:
York cannot speak, unless he wear a crown.

100. **marry:** truly ("by the Virgin Mary").

105. **As I bethink me:** now that I think of it.

107. **pale:** impale; encircle.

112. **whilst we breathe:** while we live and have the opportunity.

114. **orisons:** prayers.

118. **ill-beseeming:** unbecoming.

119. **trull:** trollop.

121. **vizard-like:** masklike.

122. **Made impudent with use of evil deeds:** so accustomed to evil deeds as to be completely shameless.

127. **type:** style; title.

A crown for York! and, lords, bow low to him.
Hold you his hands, whilst I do set it on.
[*Putting a paper crown on his head.*]
Ay, marry, sir, now looks he like a king! 100
Ay, this is he that took King Henry's chair;
And this is he was his adopted heir.
But how is it that great Plantagenet
Is crowned so soon and broke his solemn oath?
As I bethink me, you should not be King 105
Till our King Henry had shook hands with death.
And will you pale your head in Henry's glory,
And rob his temples of the diadem,
Now in his life, against your holy oath?
Oh, 'tis a fault too-too unpardonable! 110
Off with the crown; and, with the crown, his head;
And, whilst we breathe, take time to do him dead.

Cliff. That is my office, for my father's sake.

Queen M. Nay, stay: let's hear the orisons he makes.

York. She-wolf of France, but worse than wolves of France, 115
Whose tongue more poisons than the adder's tooth!
How ill-beseeming is it in thy sex
To triumph, like an Amazonian trull,
Upon their woes whom fortune captivates! 120
But that thy face is, vizard-like, unchanging,
Made impudent with use of evil deeds,
I would assay, proud Queen, to make thee blush.
To tell thee whence thou camest, of whom derived,
Were shame enough to shame thee, wert thou not shameless. 125
Thy father bears the type of King of Naples,

128. **both the Sicils:** i.e., the southern tip of Italy, including Naples, and the island of Sicily.

130. **insult:** be proud.

131. **boots:** avails.

132. **Unless the adage must be verified:** unless to verify the adage.

133. **beggars mounted run their horse to death:** the proverb comments on the waste of wealth by those unused to it.

138. **government:** disciplined conduct; decorum.

139. **abominable:** inhuman; unnatural.

142. **Septentrion:** North.

148. **remorseless:** merciless.

155. **fell:** savage.

157. **Beshrew me:** plague take me.

Of both the Sicils and Jerusalem,
Yet not so wealthy as an English yeoman.
Hath that poor monarch taught thee to insult? 130
It needs not, nor it boots thee not, proud queen,
Unless the adage must be verified,
That beggars mounted run their horse to death.
'Tis beauty that doth oft make women proud:
But, God He knows, thy share thereof is small. 135
'Tis virtue that doth make them most admired:
The contrary doth make thee wondered at.
'Tis government that makes them seem divine:
The want thereof makes thee abominable.
Thou art as opposite to every good 140
As the Antipodes are unto us,
Or as the South to the Septentrion.
O tiger's heart wrapped in a woman's hide!
How couldst thou drain the lifeblood of the child,
To bid the father wipe his eyes withal, 145
And yet be seen to bear a woman's face?
Women are soft, mild, pitiful, and flexible;
Thou stern, obdurate, flinty, rough, remorseless.
Bidst thou me rage? Why, now thou hast thy wish.
Wouldst have me weep? Why, now thou hast thy will. 150
For raging wind blows up incessant showers,
And when the rage allays, the rain begins.
These tears are my sweet Rutland's obsequies:
And every drop cries vengeance for his death,
'Gainst thee, fell Clifford, and thee, false French- 155
woman.

North. Beshrew me, but his passions move me so
That hardly can I check my eyes from tears.

163. **Hyrcania:** a region in Asia, southeast of the Caspian, reputed to contain particularly fierce tigers.
168. **heavy:** melancholy.
179. **inly:** heartily.
180. **weeping-ripe:** moved to tears.

York. That face of his the hungry cannibals
Would not have touched, would not have stained with blood: 160
But you are more inhuman, more inexorable,
Oh, ten times more, than tigers of Hyrcania.
See, ruthless queen, a hapless father's tears:
This cloth thou dipp'dst in blood of my sweet boy, 165
And I with tears do wash the blood away.
Keep thou the napkin, and go boast of this:
And if thou tellst the heavy story right,
Upon my soul, the hearers will shed tears;
Yea, even my foes will shed fast-falling tears, 170
And say, "Alas, it was a piteous deed!"
There, take the crown, and, with the crown, my curse;
And in thy need such comfort come to thee
As now I reap at thy too cruel hand!
Hard-hearted Clifford, take me from the world: 175
My soul to Heaven, my blood upon your heads!

North. Had he been slaughterman to all my kin,
I should not for my life but weep with him,
To see how inly sorrow gripes his soul.

Queen M. What, weeping-ripe, my Lord Northumberland? 180
Think but upon the wrong he did us all
And that will quickly dry thy melting tears.

Cliff. Here's for my oath, here's for my father's death. [*Stabbing him.*] 185

Queen M. And here's to right our gentle-hearted king. [*Stabbing him.*]

York. Open Thy gate of mercy, gracious God!

My soul flies through these wounds to seek out Thee.

[*Dies.*]

Queen M. Off with his head and set it on York gates; 190

So York may overlook the town of York.

Flourish. Exeunt.

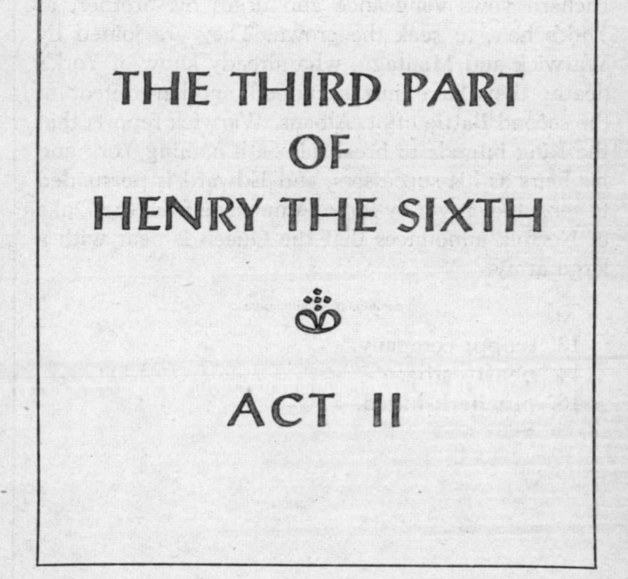

THE THIRD PART OF HENRY THE SIXTH

ACT II

[II.i.] As Edward and Richard speculate about their father's fate, they see three suns in the sky; Edward resolves to adopt three suns as his badge. A messenger brings word of the deaths of York and Rutland. Edward is despairing and tearful, but Richard vows vengeance and urges his brother, as York's heir, to seek the crown. They are joined by Warwick and Montagu, who already know of York's death; they have just sustained another defeat at the second Battle of St. Albans. Warwick reports that the King intends to break his oath naming York and his heirs as his successors, and Edward is persuaded to seize the crown by force. A message from the Duke of Norfolk announces that the Queen is near with a large army.

13. **troop:** company.
14. **neat:** cattle.
16. **pinched:** bitten.

[*ACT II*]

[Scene I. A plain near Mortimer's Cross in Herefordshire.]

A march. Enter Edward, Richard, and their power.

Edw. I wonder how our princely father 'scaped,
Or whether he be 'scaped away or no
From Clifford's and Northumberland's pursuit.
Had he been ta'en, we should have heard the news;
Had he been slain, we should have heard the news; 5
Or had he 'scaped, methinks we should have heard
The happy tidings of his good escape.
How fares my brother? Why is he so sad?
Rich. I cannot joy until I be resolved
Where our right valiant father is become. 10
I saw him in the battle range about
And watched him how he singled Clifford forth.
Methought he bore him in the thickest troop
As doth a lion in a herd of neat;
Or as a bear, encompassed round with dogs, 15
Who having pinched a few and made them cry,
The rest stand all aloof and bark at him.
So fared our father with his enemies;

24. **Trimmed:** arrayed; adorned; **younker:** youngster.

27. **racking:** scudding before the wind.

32. **figures:** prefigures; forecasts.

35. **cites:** urges.

37. **meeds:** deserts.

The Battle of Mortimer's Cross. From John Speed, *The Theatre of the Empire of Great Britain* (1627).

So fled his enemies my warlike father.
Methinks 'tis prize enough to be his son. 20
See how the morning opes her golden gates
And takes her farewell of the glorious sun!
How well resembles it the prime of youth,
Trimmed like a younker, prancing to his love!
Edw. Dazzle mine eyes, or do I see three suns? 25
Rich. Three glorious suns, each one a perfect sun;
Not separated with the racking clouds
But severed in a pale, clear-shining sky.
See, see! they join, embrace, and seem to kiss,
As if they vowed some league inviolable: 30
Now are they but one lamp, one light, one sun.
In this the heaven figures some event.
Edw. 'Tis wondrous strange, the like yet never heard of.
I think it cites us, brother, to the field, 35
That we, the sons of brave Plantagenet,
Each one already blazing by our meeds,
Should notwithstanding join our lights together
And overshine the earth as this the world.
Whate'er it bodes, henceforward will I bear 40
Upon my target three fair-shining suns.
Rich. Nay, bear three daughters: by your leave I speak it,
You love the breeder better than the male.

Enter a Messenger, blowing.

But what art thou, whose heavy looks foretell 45
Some dreadful story hanging on thy tongue?

54. **the hope of Troy:** Hector, eldest son of King Priam of Troy and the city's most renowned warrior.

56. **Hercules himself must yield to odds:** proverbial; see cut, below.

62. **high:** haughty.

72. **stay:** support.

73. **boist'rous:** violent.

Hercules, attacked by pygmies. From Geoffrey Whitney, *A Choice of Emblems* (1586).

Mess. Ah, one that was a woeful looker-on
Whenas the noble Duke of York was slain,
Your princely father and my loving lord!
Edw. Oh, speak no more, for I have heard too much. 50
Rich. Say how he died, for I will hear it all.
Mess. Environed he was with many foes
And stood against them, as the hope of Troy
Against the Greeks that would have entered Troy. 55
But Hercules himself must yield to odds;
And many strokes, though with a little ax,
Hews down and fells the hardest-timbered oak.
By many hands your father was subdued;
But only slaughtered by the ireful arm 60
Of unrelenting Clifford and the Queen,
Who crowned the gracious Duke in high despite,
Laughed in his face, and when with grief he wept,
The ruthless Queen gave him to dry his cheeks
A napkin steeped in the harmless blood 65
Of sweet young Rutland, by rough Clifford slain.
And after many scorns, many foul taunts,
They took his head and on the gates of York
They set the same; and there it doth remain,
The saddest spectacle that e'er I viewed. 70
Edw. Sweet Duke of York, our prop to lean upon,
Now thou art gone, we have no staff, no stay.
O Clifford, boist'rous Clifford! thou hast slain
The flow'r of Europe for his chivalry;
And treacherously hast thou vanquished him, 75
For hand to hand he would have vanquished thee.
Now my soul's palace is become a prison:

83. **furnace-burning:** burning like a furnace.

97. **gazing 'gainst the sun:** a habit attributed to the eagle, perhaps because it flies so high. This ability was interpreted as symbolizing the bird's royal nature.

99. **Either that is thine, or else thou wert not his:** i.e., if you do not claim the throne and kingdom, you cannot be York's legitimate son.

103. **baleful:** sorrowful.

"Many strokes fell the oak." From Claude Menestrier, *L'art des emblemes* (1684).

Ah, would she break from hence, that this my body
Might in the ground be closed up in rest!
For never henceforth shall I joy again, 80
Never, oh, never, shall I see more joy!
Rich. I cannot weep, for all my body's moisture
Scarce serves to quench my furnace-burning heart.
Nor can my tongue unload my heart's great burden,
For selfsame wind that I should speak withal 85
Is kindling coals that fires all my breast
And burns me up with flames that tears would quench.
To weep is to make less the depth of grief:
Tears then for babes; blows and revenge for me! 90
Richard, I bear thy name: I'll venge thy death,
Or die renowned by attempting it.
Edw. His name that valiant duke hath left with thee;
His dukedom and his chair with me is left. 95
Rich. Nay, if thou be that princely eagle's bird,
Show thy descent by gazing 'gainst the sun.
For chair and dukedom, throne and kingdom say;
Either that is thine, or else thou wert not his.

March. Enter Warwick, Marquess Montagu, and their army.

War. How now, fair lords! What fare? What news abroad? 100
Rich. Great lord of Warwick, if we should recount
Our baleful news and at each word's deliverance
Stab poniards in our flesh till all were told,

109. **stern:** cruel.

110. **these news:** originally **news** was a plural with the sense "new things."

111. **measure:** quantity.

114. **latest:** last.

116. **depart:** departure; death.

119. **appointed:** equipped. This line has been added from the Quarto.

121. **in my behalf along:** along by my side, for my advantage.

122. **advertised:** informed.

127. **battles joined:** forces met in battle.

128. **coldness:** apathy.

130. **spleen:** resolute courage.

Eagle gazing into the sun, emblem of royalty. From Henry Peacham, *Minerva Britanna* (1612). (See ll. 96–7 above.)

The words would add more anguish than the wounds. 105
O valiant lord, the Duke of York is slain!
Edw. O Warwick, Warwick! that Plantagenet
Which held thee dearly as his soul's redemption
Is by the stern Lord Clifford done to death.
War. Ten days ago I drowned these news in tears; 110
And now, to add more measure to your woes,
I come to tell you things sith then befall'n.
After the bloody fray at Wakefield fought,
Where your brave father breathed his latest gasp,
Tidings, as swiftly as the posts could run, 115
Were brought me of your loss and his depart.
I, then in London, keeper of the King,
Mustered my soldiers, gathered flocks of friends,
And very well appointed, as I thought,
Marched toward St. Albans to intercept the Queen, 120
Bearing the King in my behalf along;
For by my scouts I was advertised
That she was coming with a full intent
To dash our late decree in Parliament
Touching King Henry's oath and your succession. 125
Short tale to make, we at St. Albans met,
Our battles joined, and both sides fiercely fought.
But whether 'twas the coldness of the King,
Who looked full gently on his warlike queen,
That robbed my soldiers of their heated spleen; 130
Or whether 'twas report of her success;
Or more than common fear of Clifford's rigor,
Who thunders to his captives blood and death,
I cannot judge: but, to conclude with truth,
Their weapons like to lightning came and went; 135

145. **In haste, posthaste:** with all speed.

146. **marches:** borders (of Wales). The earls of March were lords of the borderlands.

147. **Making another head:** assembling another army.

150. **when came George from Burgundy:** because of their youth, both George and Richard were sent by their mother to Utrecht for safety after York was killed at Wakefield in 1460 and actually did not return until after Edward became King in 1461.

154. **kind aunt:** Isabel, wife of Philip the Good, Duke of Burgundy, must be meant; but she was the granddaughter of John of Gaunt, and hence a distant cousin of Edward rather than his aunt.

156. **'Twas odds, belike:** i.e., the odds against him must have been heavy.

163. **awful:** awe-inspiring.

Our soldiers', like the night owl's lazy flight,
Or like a lazy thresher with a flail,
Fell gently down, as if they struck their friends.
I cheered them up with justice of our cause,
With promise of high pay and great rewards. 140
But all in vain; they had no heart to fight,
And we in them no hope to win the day;
So that we fled; the King unto the Queen;
Lord George your brother, Norfolk, and myself,
In haste, posthaste are come to join with you; 145
For in the marches here we heard you were,
Making another head to fight again.

Edw. Where is the Duke of Norfolk, gentle Warwick?
And when came George from Burgundy to England? 150

War. Some six miles off the Duke is with the soldiers;
And for your brother, he was lately sent
From your kind aunt, Duchess of Burgundy,
With aid of soldiers to this needful war. 155

Rich. 'Twas odds, belike, when valiant Warwick fled.
Oft have I heard his praises in pursuit,
But ne'er till now his scandal of retire.

War. Nor now my scandal, Richard, dost thou hear; 160
For thou shalt know this strong right hand of mine
Can pluck the diadem from faint Henry's head
And wring the awful scepter from his fist
Were he as famous and as bold in war
As he is famed for mildness, peace, and prayer. 165

Rich. I know it well, Lord Warwick: blame me not.

173. **Tell:** count off with blows, like the mechanical striking of a clock.

178. **Attend:** hear.

180. **mo:** additional; other.

186. **make against:** be disadvantageous to.

192. **Via:** let's be off; **amain:** at full speed (added from the Quarto).

'Tis love I bear thy glories makes me speak.
But in this troublous time what's to be done?
Shall we go throw away our coats of steel
And wrap our bodies in black mourning gowns, 170
Numb'ring our Ave Maries with our beads?
Or shall we on the helmets of our foes
Tell our devotion with revengeful arms?
If for the last, say, "Ay," and to it, lords.

War. Why, therefore Warwick came to seek you out; 175
And therefore comes my brother Montagu.
Attend me, lords. The proud insulting Queen,
With Clifford and the haught Northumberland,
And of their feather many mo proud birds, 180
Have wrought the easy-melting King like wax.
He swore consent to your succession,
His oath enrolled in the Parliament;
And now to London all the crew are gone,
To frustrate both his oath and what beside 185
May make against the house of Lancaster.
Their power, I think, is thirty thousand strong.
Now, if the help of Norfolk and myself,
With all the friends that thou, brave Earl of March,
Amongst the loving Welshmen canst procure, 190
Will but amount to five-and-twenty thousand,
Why, Via! to London will we march amain,
And once again bestride our foaming steeds,
And once again cry, "Charge upon our foes!"
But never once again turn back and fly. 195

Rich. Ay, now methinks I hear great Warwick speak.

202. **forfend:** forbid; prevent.
219. **puissant:** powerful.
220. **craves:** requests.
221. **it sorts:** it falls out suitably; every circumstance seems to ordain a battle.

Ne'er may he live to see a sunshine day
That cries, "Retire," if Warwick bid him stay.
Edw. Lord Warwick, on thy shoulder will I lean; 200
And when thou failst—as God forbid the hour!—
Must Edward fall, which peril Heaven forfend!
War. No longer Earl of March but Duke of York.
The next degree is England's royal throne;
For King of England shalt thou be proclaimed 205
In every borough as we pass along;
And he that throws not up his cap for joy
Shall for the fault make forfeit of his head.
King Edward, valiant Richard, Montagu,
Stay we no longer, dreaming of renown, 210
But sound the trumpets and about our task.
Rich. Then, Clifford, were thy heart as hard as steel,
As thou hast shown it flinty by thy deeds,
I come to pierce it or to give thee mine.
Edw. Then strike up drums: God and St. George for us! 215

Enter a Messenger.

War. How now! what news?
Mess. The Duke of Norfolk sends you word by me,
The Queen is coming with a puissant host;
And craves your company for speedy counsel. 220
War. Why then it sorts, brave warriors, let's away.
Exeunt.

[II.ii.] At York, the Queen and Clifford exult at the sight of York's head over the gates, but the King, remembering his oath, broken through no fault of his own, tells Clifford that evil deeds never have good ends. As if to confirm the King's foreboding, a messenger announces the approach of Warwick and Edward, Duke of York, who has been proclaimed King in many towns and has gained followers in his progress through the country. The King, who might have offered to make amends to Edward, is forced by the Queen and Clifford to take no action. Edward orders the trumpets to sound for battle.

1. **brave:** splendid.
11. **lenity:** mercy.
16. **spoils:** preys upon.
21. **level:** aim.

[Scene II. Before York.]

Flourish. Enter the King, the Queen, the young Prince, Clifford, and Northumberland, with Drum and Trumpets.

Queen M. Welcome, my lord, to this brave town of York.
Yonder's the head of that archenemy
That sought to be encompassed with your crown.
Doth not the object cheer your heart, my lord? 5
King H. Ay, as the rocks cheer them that fear their wrack:
To see this sight, it irks my very soul.
Withhold revenge, dear God! 'tis not my fault,
Nor wittingly have I infringed my vow. 10
Cliff. My gracious liege, this too much lenity
And harmful pity must be laid aside.
To whom do lions cast their gentle looks?
Not to the beast that would usurp their den.
Whose hand is that the forest bear doth lick? 15
Not his that spoils her young before her face.
Who 'scapes the lurking serpent's mortal sting?
Not he that sets his foot upon her back.
The smallest worm will turn, being trodden on;
And doves will peck in safeguard of their brood. 20
Ambitious York did level at thy crown,
Thou smiling while he knit his angry brows.
He, but a duke, would have his son a king,
And raise his issue, like a loving sire;

28. **Unreasonable:** lacking in reasoning ability, like animals.

40. **fondly:** foolishly.

46. **Inferring:** mentioning.

49–50. **happy always was it for that son/ Whose father for his hoarding went to hell:** a proverbial idea.

Thou, being a king, blest with a goodly son, 25
Didst yield consent to disinherit him,
Which argued thee a most unloving father.
Unreasonable creatures feed their young;
And though man's face be fearful to their eyes,
Yet, in protection of their tender ones, 30
Who hath not seen them, even with those wings
Which sometime they have used with fearful flight,
Make war with him that climbed unto their nest,
Offering their own lives in their young's defense?
For shame, my liege, make them your precedent! 35
Were it not pity that this goodly boy
Should lose his birthright by his father's fault,
And long hereafter say unto his child,
"What my great-grandfather and grandsire got
My careless father fondly gave away"? 40
Ah, what a shame were this! Look on the boy
And let his manly face, which promiseth
Successful fortune, steel thy melting heart
To hold thine own and leave thine own with him.

King H. Full well hath Clifford played the orator, 45
Inferring arguments of mighty force.
But, Clifford, tell me, didst thou never hear
That things ill-got had ever bad success?
And happy always was it for that son
Whose father for his hoarding went to hell? 50
I'll leave my son my virtuous deeds behind;
And would my father had left me no more!
For all the rest is held at such a rate
As brings a thousandfold more care to keep
Than in possession any jot of pleasure. 55

62. **presently:** at once.

67. **apparent:** heir apparent.

69. **toward:** promising.

75. **Darraign your battle:** dispose your forces in battle array.

Ah, cousin York! would thy best friends did know
How it doth grieve me that thy head is here!
Queen M. My lord, cheer up your spirits: our foes are nigh,
And this soft courage makes your followers faint. 60
You promised knighthood to our forward son:
Unsheathe your sword and dub him presently.
Edward, kneel down.
King H. Edward Plantagenet, arise a knight;
And learn this lesson, draw thy sword in right. 65
Prince. My gracious father, by your kingly leave,
I'll draw it as apparent to the crown,
And in that quarrel use it to the death.
Cliff. Why, that is spoken like a toward prince.

Enter a Messenger.

Mess. Royal commanders, be in readiness: 70
For with a band of thirty thousand men
Comes Warwick, backing of the Duke of York,
And in the towns, as they do march along,
Proclaims him King, and many fly to him.
Darraign your battle, for they are at hand. 75
Cliff. I would your Highness would depart the field.
The Queen hath best success when you are absent.
Queen M. Ay, good my lord, and leave us to our fortune.
King H. Why, that's my fortune too; therefore I'll stay. 80
North. Be it with resolution then to fight.

89. **bide:** endure; **mortal:** deadly.

90. **rate:** scold; **minions:** paramours.

104. **any he the proudest of thy sort:** anyone of your company, no matter how valiant.

Prince. My royal father, cheer these noble lords,
And hearten those that fight in your defense.
Unsheathe your sword, good father: cry, "St. George!" 85

March. Enter Edward, George, Richard, Warwick, Norfolk, Montagu, and Soldiers.

Edw. Now, perjured Henry! wilt thou kneel for grace
And set thy diadem upon my head,
Or bide the mortal fortune of the field?
Queen M. Go, rate thy minions, proud insulting boy! 90
Becomes it thee to be thus bold in terms
Before thy sovereign and thy lawful king?
Edw. I am his king, and he should bow his knee.
I was adopted heir by his consent: 95
Since when, his oath is broke; for, as I hear,
You, that are King, though he do wear the crown,
Have caused him, by new act of Parliament,
To blot out me and put his own son in.
Cliff. And reason too: 100
Who should succeed the father but the son?
Rich. Are you there, butcher? Oh, I cannot speak!
Cliff. Ay, Crookback, here I stand to answer thee,
Or any he the proudest of thy sort.
Rich. 'Twas you that killed young Rutland, was it not? 105
Cliff. Ay, and old York, and yet not satisfied.
Rich. For God's sake, lords, give signal to the fight.

From Olaus Magnus, *Historia de gentibus septentrionalibus* (1555).

War. What sayst thou, Henry, wilt thou yield the crown? 110

Queen M. Why, how now, long-tongued Warwick! dare you speak?
When you and I met at St. Albans last,
Your legs did better service than your hands.

War. Then 'twas my turn to fly, and now 'tis thine. 115

Cliff. You said so much before, and yet you fled.

War. 'Twas not your valor, Clifford, drove me thence.

North. No, nor your manhood that durst make you stay. 120

Rich. Northumberland, I hold thee reverently.
Break off the parley; for scarce I can refrain
The execution of my big-swol'n heart
Upon that Clifford, that cruel child-killer.

Cliff. I slew thy father, callst thou him a child? 125

Rich. Ay, like a dastard and a treacherous coward,
As thou didst kill our tender brother Rutland;
But ere sun set I'll make thee curse the deed.

King H. Have done with words, my lords, and hear me speak. 130

Queen M. Defy them then, or else hold close thy lips.

King H. I prithee, give no limits to my tongue:
I am a king, and privileged to speak.

Cliff. My liege, the wound that bred this meeting here 135
Cannot be cured by words: therefore be still.

Rich. Then, executioner, unsheathe thy sword.
By Him that made us all, I am resolved

142. **broke their fasts:** breakfasted.
148. **got:** begot.
149. **wot:** know.
151. **stigmatic:** deformity.
152. **Destinies:** the classical Fates.
156. **channel:** street gutter.
157–58. **extraught:** extracted; derived by birth.
160. **A wisp of straw:** traditional sign of a scold.
162. **callet:** scolding beggarwoman.
164. **Menelaus:** betrayed husband of Helen; i.e., Margaret may have betrayed her husband, as Menelaus was betrayed by Helen. There were rumors that Henry was not the father of the Prince of Wales.

That Clifford's manhood lies upon his tongue. 140
Edw. Say, Henry, shall I have my right, or no?
A thousand men have broke their fasts today
That ne'er shall dine unless thou yield the crown.
War. If thou deny, their blood upon thy head;
For York in justice puts his armor on. 145
Prince. If that be right which Warwick says is right,
There is no wrong, but everything is right.
Rich. Whoever got thee, there thy mother stands;
For, well I wot, thou hast thy mother's tongue.
Queen M. But thou art neither like thy sire nor dam; 150
But like a foul misshapen stigmatic,
Marked by the Destinies to be avoided,
As venom toads, or lizards' dreadful stings.
Rich. Iron of Naples hid with English gilt,
Whose father bears the title of a King— 155
As if a channel should be called the sea—
Shamest thou not, knowing whence thou art extraught,
To let thy tongue detect thy baseborn heart?
Edw. A wisp of straw were worth a thousand crowns, 160
To make this shameless callet know herself.
Helen of Greece was fairer far than thou,
Although thy husband may be Menelaus;
And ne'er was Agamemnon's brother wronged 165
By that false woman as this King by thee.
His father reveled in the heart of France,
And tamed the King, and made the Dauphin stoop;
And had he matched according to his state,
He might have kept that glory to this day; 170

172. **graced thy poor sire with his bridal day:** i.e., made the poverty-stricken father a present of his daughter's bridal, since no dowry was demanded.

176. **broached:** started (from broaching—piercing—a barrel of ale).

179. **slipped:** neglected.

182. **increase:** profit.

184. **something:** somewhat.

189. **longer conference:** further conversation.

But when he took a beggar to his bed,
And graced thy poor sire with his bridal day,
Even then that sunshine brewed a show'r for him
That washed his father's fortunes forth of France
And heaped sedition on his crown at home. 175
For what hath broached this tumult but thy pride?
Hadst thou been meek, our title still had slept;
And we, in pity of the gentle King,
Had slipped our claim until another age.
Geo. But when we saw our sunshine made thy spring, 180
And that thy summer bred us no increase,
We set the ax to thy usurping root;
And though the edge hath something hit ourselves,
Yet, know thou, since we have begun to strike, 185
We'll never leave till we have hewn thee down
Or bathed thy growing with our heated bloods.
Edw. And, in this resolution, I defy thee;
Not willing any longer conference,
Since thou denied'st the gentle King to speak. 190
Sound trumpets! Let our bloody colors wave!
And either victory, or else a grave.
Queen M. Stay, Edward.
Edw. No, wrangling woman, we'll no longer stay:
These words will cost ten thousand lives this day. 195
Exeunt.

[II.iii.] Although the battle is going against Edward and his allies, they resolve to fight until they conquer or die.

1. **Forspent:** completely exhausted.

From John Speed, *The Theatre of the Empire of Great Britain* (1627).

[Scene III. A field of battle between Towton and Saxton in Yorkshire.]

Alarum. Excursions. Enter Warwick.

War. Forspent with toil, as runners with a race,
I lay me down a little while to breathe;
For strokes received and many blows repaid
Have robbed my strong-knit sinews of their strength,
And spite of spite needs must I rest awhile. 5

Enter Edward, running.

Edw. Smile, gentle Heaven! or strike, ungentle Death!
For this world frowns, and Edward's sun is clouded.
War. How now, my lord! what hap? What hope of good? 10

Enter George.

Geo. Our hap is loss, our hope but sad despair;
Our ranks are broke, and ruin follows us.
What counsel give you? Whither shall we fly?
Edw. Bootless is flight, they follow us with wings;
And weak we are and cannot shun pursuit. 15

Enter Richard.

18. **brother:** Warwick had a nephew, John Neville, who was killed at Towton. The nephew is probably confused here with Warwick's brother of the same name, who was killed later, at Barnet.

21. **dismal:** boding disaster.

27. **because I will not:** i.e., so that I cannot.

45. **take leave:** say good-by.

Rich. Ah, Warwick, why hast thou withdrawn thyself?
Thy brother's blood thc thirsty carth hath drunk,
Broached with the steely point of Clifford's lance;
And in the very pangs of death he cried, 20
Like to a dismal clangor heard from far,
"Warwick, revenge! Brother, revenge my death!"
So, underneath the belly of their steeds,
That stained their fetlocks in his smoking blood,
The noble gentleman gave up the ghost. 25

War. Then let the earth be drunken with our blood:
I'll kill my horse, because I will not fly.
Why stand we like soft-hearted women here,
Wailing our losses, whiles the foe doth rage;
And look upon, as if the tragedy 30
Were played in jest by counterfeiting actors?
Here on my knee I vow to God above,
I'll never pause again, never stand still,
Till either death hath closed these eyes of mine
Or fortune given me measure of revenge. 35

Edw. O Warwick, I do bend my knee with thine;
And in this vow do chain my soul to thine!
And, ere my knee rise from the earth's cold face,
I throw my hands, mine eyes, my heart to Thee,
Thou setter-up and plucker-down of kings, 40
Beseeching Thee, if with Thy will it stands
That to my foes this body must be prey,
Yet that Thy brazen gates of Heaven may ope
And give sweet passage to my sinful soul!
Now, lords, take leave until we meet again, 45
Where'er it be, in Heaven or in earth.

61. **Forslow:** delay.

[II.iv.] Richard engages Clifford in combat, but when Warwick appears, Clifford makes his escape. Richard forbids Warwick to pursue Clifford, whom he has singled out for his own prey.

Rich. Brother, give me thy hand; and, gentle Warwick,
Let me embrace thee in my weary arms.
I, that did never weep, now melt with woe 50
That winter should cut off our springtime so.
War. Away, away! Once more, sweet lords, farewell.
Geo. Yet let us all together to our troops,
And give them leave to fly that will not stay; 55
And call them pillars that will stand to us;
And, if we thrive, promise them such rewards
As victors wear at the Olympian games.
This may plant courage in their quailing breasts;
For yet is hope of life and victory. 60
Forslow no longer, make we hence amain.
Exeunt.

[Scene IV. Another part of the field.]

Excursions. Enter Richard and Clifford.

Rich. Now, Clifford, I have singled thee alone:
Suppose this arm is for the Duke of York,
And this for Rutland; both bound to revenge,
Wert thou environed with a brazen wall.
Cliff. Now, Richard, I am with thee here alone. 5
This is the hand that stabbed thy father York
And this the hand that slew thy brother Rutland;
And here's the heart that triumphs in their death

11. **have at thee:** defend thyself.
12. **chase:** quarry.

[II.v.] King Henry, ordered by the Queen and Clifford to leave the battlefield because he disheartens the men, muses on the miserable life of a king and longs for the homely pleasures of a shepherd's life. As he sits apart, he witnesses scenes that epitomize the horrors of civil war: a son discovers that the enemy he has killed and is about to rob is his father; and a father discovers that he has killed his son. Henry's grieving over his country's woe is interrupted by his wife and son, who urge him to fly toward Scotland. The Lancastrian army is routed, and Edward and Richard pursue them closely.

---

13. **poise:** balance.
17. **chid:** scolded.

And cheers these hands that slew thy sire and brother
To execute the like upon thyself; 10
And so, have at thee!

They fight. Warwick comes. Clifford flies.

Rich. Nay, Warwick, single out some other chase;
For I myself will hunt this wolf to death.

Exeunt.

[Scene V. Another part of the field.]

Alarum. Enter King Henry, alone.

King H. This battle fares like to the morning's war,
When dying clouds contend with growing light,
What time the shepherd, blowing of his nails,
Can neither call it perfect day nor night.
Now sways it this way, like a mighty sea 5
Forced by the tide to combat with the wind;
Now sways it that way, like the selfsame sea
Forced to retire by fury of the wind:
Sometime the flood prevails, and then the wind;
Now one the better, then another best; 10
Both tugging to be victors, breast to breast,
Yet neither conqueror nor conquered:
So is the equal poise of this fell war.
Here on this molehill will I sit me down.
To whom God will, there be the victory! 15
For Margaret my queen, and Clifford too,
Have chid me from the battle, swearing both

22. **homely swain:** simple peasant.
24. **dials:** clocks.
36. **ean:** give birth.
43. **silly:** harmless.

They prosper best of all when I am thence.
Would I were dead! if God's good will were so;
For what is in this world but grief and woe? 20
O God! methinks it were a happy life
To be no better than a homely swain;
To sit upon a hill, as I do now,
To carve out dials quaintly, point by point,
Thereby to see the minutes how they run, 25
How many makes the hour full complete;
How many hours brings about the day;
How many days will finish up the year;
How many years a mortal man may live.
When this is known, then to divide the times: 30
So many hours must I tend my flock;
So many hours must I take my rest;
So many hours must I contemplate;
So many hours must I sport myself;
So many days my ewes have been with young; 35
So many weeks ere the poor fools will ean;
So many years ere I shall shear the fleece.
So minutes, hours, days, months, and years,
Passed over to the end they were created,
Would bring white hairs unto a quiet grave. 40
Ah, what a life were this! how sweet! how lovely!
Gives not the hawthorn bush a sweeter shade
To shepherds looking on their silly sheep
Than doth a rich embroidered canopy
To kings that fear their subjects' treachery? 45
Oh, yes, it doth; a thousandfold it doth.
And, to conclude, the shepherd's homely curds,
His cold thin drink out of his leather bottle,

51. **delicates:** delicacies.
53. **curious:** elaborate; exquisitely wrought.
58. **haply:** perhaps.
75. **abide:** withstand; endure.

Emblem of civil war. From Geoffrey Whitney, *A Choice of Emblems* (1586). Whitney's verse reads, in part:
"Intestine strife is fearful most of all:
This makes the son to cut his father's throat. . . .
This Rome did feel; this Germany did taste;
And oftentimes this noble land did waste."

His wonted sleep under a fresh tree's shade,
All which secure and sweetly he enjoys, 50
Is far beyond a prince's delicates,
His viands sparkling in a golden cup,
His body couched in a curious bed,
When care, mistrust, and treason waits on him.

Alarum. Enter a Son that hath killed his father, [*dragging in the body*].

Son. Ill blows the wind that profits nobody. 55
This man, whom hand to hand I slew in fight,
May be possessed with some store of crowns;
And I, that haply take them from him now,
May yet ere night yield both my life and them
To some man else, as this dead man doth me. 60
Who's this? O God! it is my father's face,
Whom in this conflict I, unwares, have killed.
O heavy times, begetting such events!
From London by the King was I pressed forth;
My father, being the Earl of Warwick's man, 65
Came on the part of York, pressed by his master;
And I, who at his hands received my life,
Have by my hands of life bereaved him.
Pardon me, God, I knew not what I did!
And pardon, father, for I knew not thee! 70
My tears shall wipe away these bloody marks;
And no more words till they have flowed their fill.

King H. O piteous spectacle! O bloody times!
Whiles lions war and battle for their dens,
Poor harmless lambs abide their enmity. 75

89. **fell:** savage; deadly.
90. **Erroneous:** wicked.
93. **late:** recently.
96. **ruthful:** full of occasion for ruth (pity).

Weep, wretched man, I'll aid thee tear for tear;
And let our hearts and eyes, like civil war,
Be blind with tears, and break o'ercharged with grief.

Enter a Father that hath killed his son, [bringing in the body].

Father. Thou that so stoutly hast resisted me,
Give me thy gold, if thou hast any gold; 80
For I have bought it with an hundred blows.
But let me see: is this our foeman's face?
Ah, no, no, no, it is mine only son!
Ah, boy, if any life be left in thee,
Throw up thine eye! See, see what showers arise, 85
Blown with the windy tempest of my heart;
Upon thy wounds, that kills mine eye and heart!
Oh, pity, God, this miserable age!
What stratagems, how fell, how butcherly,
Erroneous, mutinous, and unnatural, 90
This deadly quarrel daily doth beget!
O boy, thy father gave thee life too soon,
And hath bereft thee of thy life too late!
King H. Woe above woe! grief more than common grief! 95
O that my death would stay these ruthful deeds!
Oh, pity, pity, gentle Heaven, pity!
The red rose and the white are on his face,
The fatal colors of our striving houses:
The one his purple blood right well resembles; 100
The other his pale cheeks, methinks, presenteth.
Wither one rose and let the other flourish;

110. **Misthink:** condemn.

121. **obsequious:** dutiful in performing funeral rites.

123. **Priam:** the King of Troy had fifty sons.

126. **overgone:** overcome.

If you contend, a thousand lives must wither.

Son. How will my mother for a father's death
Take on with me and ne'er be satisfied! 105

Father. How will my wife for slaughter of my son
Shed seas of tears and ne'er be satisfied!

King H. How will the country for these woeful chances
Misthink the King and not be satisfied! 110

Son. Was ever son so rued a father's death?

Father. Was ever father so bemoaned his son?

King H. Was ever king so grieved for subjects' woe?
Much is your sorrow; mine ten times so much.

Son. I'll bear thee hence, where I may weep my fill. 115

[*Exit with the body.*]

Father. These arms of mine shall be thy winding sheet;
My heart, sweet boy, shall be thy sepulcher,
For from my heart thine image ne'er shall go;
My sighing breast shall be thy funeral bell; 120
And so obsequious will thy father be,
Even for the loss of thee, having no more,
As Priam was for all his valiant sons.
I'll bear thee hence; and let them fight that will,
For I have murdered where I should not kill. 125

Exit [*with the body*].

King H. Sad-hearted men, much overgone with care,
Here sits a king more woeful than you are.

Alarums. Excursions. Enter Queen [*Margaret,*] *the Prince* [*of Wales,*] *and Exeter.*

[II.vi.] Young Clifford dies of many wounds and is found by Edward and his party. Warwick suggests that Clifford's head be placed over the gates of York in place of the Duke's. Edward creates Richard Duke of Gloucester and George Duke of Clarence. Richard protests that the title of Duke of Gloucester is unlucky, but Warwick scoffs at this idea and urges them on to London to seize the fruits of their victory.

---

5. **My love and fear:** both love and fear of me.
7. **misproud:** proud and presumptuous.

Prince. Fly, father, fly! for all your friends are fled,
And Warwick rages like a chafed bull. 130
Away! for death doth hold us in pursuit.

Queen M. Mount you, my lord; toward Berwick post amain:
Edward and Richard, like a brace of greyhounds,
Having the fearful flying hare in sight, 135
With fiery eyes sparkling for very wrath,
And bloody steel grasped in their ireful hands,
Are at our backs; and therefore hence amain.

Exe. Away! for vengeance comes along with them.
Nay, stay not to expostulate, make speed; 140
Or else come after: I'll away before.

King H. Nay, take me with thee, good sweet Exeter.
Not that I fear to stay, but love to go
Whither the Queen intends. Forward, away!

Exeunt.

[Scene VI. Another part of the field.]

A loud alarum. Enter Clifford, wounded.

Cliff. Here burns my candle out; ay, here it dies,
Which, whiles it lasted, gave King Henry light.
O Lancaster, I fear thy overthrow
More than my body's parting with my soul!
My love and fear glued many friends to thee; 5
And, now I fall, thy tough commixtures melts,
Impairing Henry, strength'ning misproud York.

8. **The common people swarm like summer flies:** from the Quarto.

12. **check:** control.

14. **swayed:** ruled.

24. **hold out:** sustain.

27. **The air hath got into my deadly wounds:** proverbially, "Fresh air is death for the diseased or wounded man"; hence, the wounds are made deadly by their exposure to air.

28. **effuse:** effusion; spilling.

31. **breathe:** rest.

The common people swarm like summer flies;
And whither fly the gnats but to the sun?
And who shines now but Henry's enemies? 10
O Phoebus, hadst thou never given consent
That Phaëthon should check thy fiery steeds,
Thy burning car never had scorched the earth!
And, Henry, hadst thou swayed as kings should do,
Or as thy father and his father did, 15
Giving no ground unto the house of York,
They never then had sprung like summer flies;
I and ten thousand in this luckless realm
Had left no mourning widows for our death;
And thou this day hadst kept thy chair in peace. 20
For what doth cherish weeds but gentle air?
And what makes robbers bold but too much lenity?
Bootless are plaints, and cureless are my wounds;
No way to fly, nor strength to hold out flight.
The foe is merciless and will not pity; 25
For at their hands I have deserved no pity.
The air hath got into my deadly wounds,
And much effuse of blood doth make me faint.
Come, York and Richard, Warwick and the rest;
I stabbed your fathers' bosoms, split my breast. 30
[*He faints.*]

Alarum and retreat. Enter Edward, George, Richard, Montagu, Warwick, and Soldiers.

Edw. Now breathe we, lords: good fortune bids us pause
And smooth the frowns of war with peaceful looks.

37. **stem:** make headway against.

45. **departing:** parting.

59. **Measure for measure must be answered:** proverbial.

Some troops pursue the bloody-minded Queen,
That led calm Henry, though he were a king, 35
As doth a sail, filled with a fretting gust,
Command an argosy to stem the waves.
But think you, lords, that Clifford fled with them?
War. No, 'tis impossible he should escape;
For, though before his face I speak the words, 40
Your brother Richard marked him for the grave:
And wheresoe'er he is, he's surely dead.
Clifford groans, [and dies].
Rich. Whose soul is that which takes her heavy leave?
A deadly groan, like life and death's departing. 45
See who it is.
Edw. And, now the battle's ended,
If friend or foe, let him be gently used.
Rich. Revoke that doom of mercy, for 'tis Clifford;
Who, not contented that he lopped the branch 50
In hewing Rutland when his leaves put forth,
But set his murd'ring knife unto the root
From whence that tender spray did sweetly spring—
I mean our princely father, Duke of York.
War. From off the gates of York fetch down the head, 55
Your father's head, which Clifford placed there;
Instead whereof let this supply the room:
Measure for measure must be answered.
Edw. Bring forth that fatal screech owl to our house, 60
That nothing sung but death to us and ours.
Now death shall stop his dismal threat'ning sound,

73. **eager:** sharp.

80. **fence:** protect.

81–2. **wast wont:** were accustomed.

83–4. **the world goes hard:** i.e., the world is not turning in its usual manner; something is very amiss.

94. **rear:** erect.

And his ill-boding tongue no more shall speak.
War. I think his understanding is bereft. 65
Speak, Clifford, dost thou know who speaks to thee?
Dark cloudy death o'ershades his beams of life,
And he nor sees nor hears us what we say.
Rich. Oh, would he did! and so perhaps he doth:
'Tis but his policy to counterfeit, 70
Because he would avoid such bitter taunts
Which in the time of death he gave our father.
Geo. If so thou thinkst, vex him with eager words.
Rich. Clifford, ask mercy and obtain no grace.
Edw. Clifford, repent in bootless penitence. 75
War. Clifford, devise excuses for thy faults.
Geo. While we devise fell tortures for thy faults.
Rich. Thou didst love York, and I am son to York.
Edw. Thou pitiedst Rutland; I will pity thee.
Geo. Where's Captain Margaret, to fence you now? 80
War. They mock thee, Clifford: swear as thou wast wont.
Rich. What, not an oath? Nay, then the world goes hard,
When Clifford cannot spare his friends an oath. 85
I know by that he's dead; and, by my soul,
If this right hand would buy two hours' life,
That I in all despite might rail at him,
This hand should chop it off and with the issuing blood 90
Stifle the villain, whose unstanched thirst
York and young Rutland could not satisfy.
War. Ay, but he's dead: off with the traitor's head,
And rear it in the place your father's stands.

98. **Lady Bona:** Bona of Savoy, sister-in-law of Louis XI of France.

103. **offend:** injure.

116. **Gloucester's dukedom is too ominous:** Humphrey of Gloucester, the last Duke, was charged with treason and died under suspicious circumstances; while the previous holder of the title, Thomas of Woodstock, seventh son of Edward III, was murdered at the instigation of Richard II.

And now to London with triumphant march, 95
There to be crowned England's royal King:
From whence shall Warwick cut the sea to France
And ask the Lady Bona for thy queen.
So shalt thou sinew both these lands together;
And, having France thy friend, thou shalt not dread 100
The scattered foe that hopes to rise again;
For though they cannot greatly sting to hurt,
Yet look to have them buzz to offend thine ears.
First will I see the coronation;
And then to Brittany I'll cross the sea, 105
To effect this marriage, so it please my lord.

Edw. Even as thou wilt, sweet Warwick, let it be;
For in thy shoulder do I build my seat,
And never will I undertake the thing
Wherein thy counsel and consent is wanting. 110
Richard, I will create thee Duke of Gloucester,
And George, of Clarence. Warwick, as ourself,
Shall do and undo as him pleaseth best.

Rich. Let me be Duke of Clarence, George of Gloucester; 115
For Gloucester's dukedom is too ominous.

War. Tut, that's a foolish observation:
Richard, be Duke of Gloucester. Now to London,
To see these honors in possession.

Exeunt.

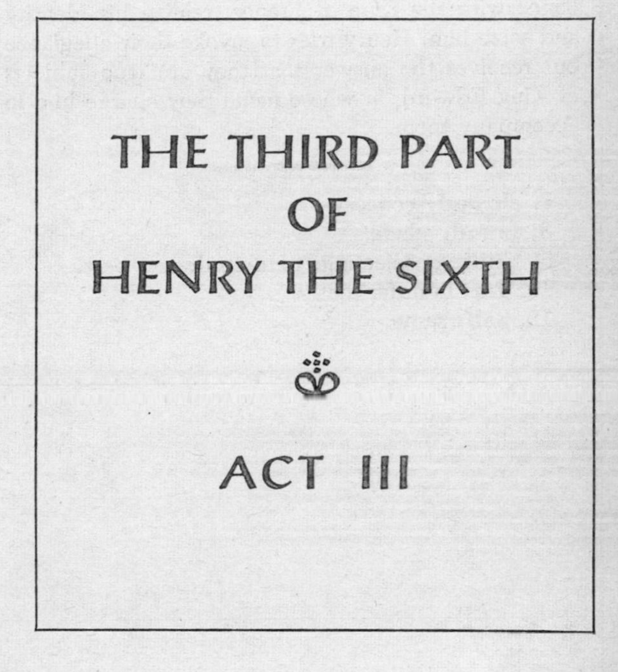
THE THIRD PART
OF
HENRY THE SIXTH
ACT III

[III.i.] King Henry has crept back from the Scottish border to take a wistful view of his country. Two woodsmen, who hear him speak of the Queen and Warwick, both of whom have gone to seek alliance with the King of France, realize his identity and seize him. Henry tries to invoke their allegiance but receives the answer that they are true subjects of King Edward, in whose name they charge him to accompany them.

1. **shroud:** conceal.
3. **laund:** glade.
5. **Culling:** selecting; **principal:** i.e., best.
10. **for:** in order that.
12. **self:** same.

[*ACT III*]

[Scene I. A forest in the North of England.]

Enter [*two Keepers,*] *with crossbows in their hands.*

1. Keep. Under this thick-grown brake we'll shroud ourselves;
For through this laund anon the deer will come;
And in this covert will we make our stand,
Culling the principal of all the deer. 5
2. Keep. I'll stay above the hill, so both may shoot.
1. Keep. That cannot be: the noise of thy crossbow
Will scare the herd, and so my shoot is lost.
Here stand we both, and aim we at the best.
And, for the time shall not seem tedious, 10
I'll tell thee what befell me on a day
In this self place where now we mean to stand.
2. Keep. Here comes a man; let's stay till he be past.

Enter King Henry, [*disguised,*] *with a prayer book.*

King H. From Scotland am I stol'n, even of pure love, 15
To greet mine own land with my wishful sight.

22. **redress:** satisfaction (of a grievance); **of:** from.

24–5. **keeper's fee:** the reward given the huntsman.

26. **quondam:** onetime; former.

38. **prince:** ruler.

No, Harry, Harry, 'tis no land of thine:
Thy place is filled, thy sceptre wrung from thee,
Thy balm washed off wherewith thou wast anointed.
No bending knee will call thee Caesar now, 20
No humble suitors press to speak for right,
No, not a man comes for redress of thee;
For how can I help them and not myself?

1. Keep. Ay, here's a deer whose skin's a keeper's fee. 25
This is the quondam King: let's seize upon him.

King H. Let me embrace thee, sour adversity,
For wise men say it is the wisest course.

2. Keep. Why linger we? Let us lay hands upon him.

1. Keep. Forbear awhile: we'll hear a little more. 30

King H. My queen and son are gone to France for aid;
And, as I hear, the great commanding Warwick
Is thither gone to crave the French king's sister
To wife for Edward. If this news be true, 35
Poor queen and son, your labor is but lost;
For Warwick is a subtle orator,
And Lewis a prince soon won with moving words.
By this account then Margaret may win him;
For she's a woman to be pitied much. 40
Her sighs will make a batt'ry in his breast;
Her tears will pierce into a marble heart;
The tiger will be mild whiles she doth mourn;
And Nero will be tainted with remorse
To hear and see her plaints, her brinish tears. 45
Ay, but she's come to beg, Warwick, to give:
She, on his left side, craving aid for Henry;

52. **smooths:** smooths over with plausible arguments.

55. **what else:** anything else desired.

He, on his right, asking a wife for Edward.
She weeps and says her Henry is deposed;
He smiles and says his Edward is installed; 50
That she, poor wretch, for grief can speak no more;
Whiles Warwick tells his title, smooths the wrong,
Inferreth arguments of mighty strength,
And in conclusion wins the King from her
With promise of his sister and what else, 55
To strengthen and support King Edward's place.
O Margaret, thus 'twill be; and thou, poor soul,
Art then forsaken, as thou wentst forlorn!

2. *Keep.* Say, what art thou that talkst of kings and queens? 60

King H. More than I seem, and less than I was born to:
A man at least, for less I should not be;
And men may talk of kings, and why not I?

2. *Keep.* Ay, but thou talkst as if thou wert a king. 65

King H. Why, so I am, in mind; and that's enough.

2. *Keep.* But, if thou be a king, where is thy crown?

King H. My crown is in my heart, not on my head;
Not decked with diamonds and Indian stones
Nor to be seen: my crown is called content: 70
A crown it is that seldom kings enjoy.

2. *Keep.* Well, if you be a king crowned with content,
Your crown content and you must be contented
To go along with us; for, as we think, 75
You are the king King Edward hath deposed;
And we, his subjects sworn in all allegiance,
Will apprehend you as his enemy.

King H. But did you never swear and break an oath? 80
2. Keep. No, never such an oath: nor will not now.
King H. Where did you dwell when I was King of England?
2. Keep. Here in this country, where we now remain. 85
King H. I was anointed King at nine months old;
My father and my grandfather were kings,
And you were sworn true subjects unto me:
And tell me, then, have you not broke your oaths?
1. Keep. No; 90
For we were subjects but while you were King.
King H. Why, am I dead? Do I not breathe a man?
Ah, simple men, you know not what you swear!
Look, as I blow this feather from my face,
And as the air blows it to me again, 95
Obeying with my wind when I do blow,
And yielding to another when it blows,
Commanded always by the greater gust;
Such is the lightness of you common men.
But do not break your oaths; for of that sin 100
My mild entreaty shall not make you guilty.
Go where you will, the King shall be commanded;
And be you kings, command and I'll obey.
1. Keep. We are true subjects to the King, King Edward. 105
King H. So would you be again to Henry,
If he were seated as King Edward is.
1. Keep. We charge you, in God's name, and the King's,

[III.ii.] As Richard and George look on, King Edward hears the petition of the Widow Grey, whose husband was killed at St. Albans, that his lands be restored to her and her children. Much smitten with the lady's beauty, Edward asks her to be his mistress, but she refuses. Her grace and modesty so impress Edward that he determines to marry her. Edward's brothers treat his decision as a jest. Richard reveals in a soliloquy that his love for his brother is mere pretense and that his every thought is directed toward gaining the crown for himself.

2. **Sir Richard Grey:** actually, Elizabeth Woodville's husband was Sir John Grey, who was killed at St. Albans in 1461, fighting on the Lancastrian side. His lands were seized for his treasonable action when Edward became King.

16. **keeps the wind:** keeps to windward of her, like a hunter stalking a deer.

To go with us unto the officers. 110

King H. In God's name, lead; your king's name be obeyed:
And what God will, that let your king perform;
And what He will, I humbly yield unto.

Exeunt.

[Scene II. London. The palace.]

Enter King Edward, Gloucester, Clarence, Lady Grey.

King Edw. Brother of Gloucester, at St. Albans field
This lady's husband, Sir Richard Grey, was slain,
His land then seized on by the conqueror.
Her suit is now to repossess those lands;
Which we in justice cannot well deny, 5
Because in quarrel of the house of York
The worthy gentleman did lose his life.

Glou. Your Highness shall do well to grant her suit:
It were dishonor to deny it her.

King Edw. It were no less; but yet I'll make a pause. 10

Glou. [*Aside to Clarence*] Yea, is it so?
I see the lady hath a thing to grant
Before the King will grant her humble suit.

Clar. [*Aside to Gloucester*] He knows the game: how true he keeps the wind! 15

Glou. [*Aside to Clarence*] Silence!

23–4. **warrant:** guarantee.

25. **And if:** if.

26. **catch a blow:** be sexually assaulted.

33–4. **beg a child:** i.e., as one might sue to the Court of Wards for the guardianship of a wealthy minor.

43. **give us leave:** grant us privacy; leave us alone.

46. **you will have leave:** i.e., women will be permissive of his advances.

SD 47. **retire:** i.e., they move out of earshot but can still observe the interview.

King Edw. Widow, we will consider of your suit;
And come some other time to know our mind.

Lady G. Right gracious lord, I cannot brook delay: 20
May it please your Highness to resolve me now;
And what your pleasure is, shall satisfy me.

Glou. [*Aside to Clarence*] Ay, widow? then I'll warrant you all your lands,
And if what pleases him shall pleasure you. 25
Fight closer, or, good faith, you'll catch a blow.

Clar. [*Aside to Gloucester*] I fear her not, unless she chance to fall.

Glou. [*Aside to Clarence*] God forbid that; for he'll take vantages. 30

King Edw. How many children hast thou, widow? tell me.

Clar. [*Aside to Gloucester*] I think he means to beg a child of her.

Glou. [*Aside to Clarence*] Nay, then whip me: he'll rather give her two. 35

Lady G. Three, my most gracious lord.

Glou. [*Aside to Clarence*] You shall have four, if you'll be ruled by him.

King Edw. 'Twere pity they should lose their father's lands. 40

Lady G. Be pitiful, dread lord, and grant it then.

King Edw. Lords, give us leave: I'll try this widow's wit.

Glou. [*Aside to Clarence*] Ay, good leave have you; for you will have leave, 45
Till youth take leave and leave you to the crutch.

[*Gloucester and Clarence retire.*]

65. boon: favor.

King Edw. Now tell me, madam, do you love your ohildron?

Lady G. Ay, full as dearly as I love myself. 50

King Edw. And would you not do much to do them good?

Lady G. To do them good, I would sustain some harm.

King Edw. Then get your husband's lands, to do them good. 55

Lady G. Therefor I came unto your Majesty.

Kind Edw. I'll tell you how these lands are to be got.

Lady G. So shall you bind me to your Highness' service. 60

King Edw. What service wilt thou do me, if I give thom?

Lady G. What you command that rests in me to do.

King Edw. But you will take exceptions to my boon. 65

Lady G. No, gracious lord, except I cannot do it.

King Edw. Ay, but thou canst do what I mean to ask.

Lady G. Why, then I will do what your Grace commands. 70

Glou. [*Aside to Clarence*] He plies her hard; and much rain wears the marble.

Clar. [*Aside to Gloucester*] As red as fire! nay, then her wax must melt.

Lady G. Why stops my lord? Shall I not hear my task? 75

King Edw. An easy task; 'tis but to love a king.

106. **honesty:** chastity.

Lady G. That's soon performed, because I am a subject.

King Edw. Why, then, thy husband's lands I freely give thee. 80

Lady G. I take my leave with many thousand thanks.

Glou. [*Aside to Clarence*] The match is made; she seals it with a curtsy. 85

King Edw. But stay thee, 'tis the fruits of love I mean.

Lady G. The fruits of love I mean, my loving liege.

King Edw. Ay, but, I fear me, in another sense.
What love, thinkst thou, I sue so much to get? 90

Lady G. My love till death, my humble thanks, my prayers;
That love which virtue begs and virtue grants.

King Edw. No, by my troth, I did not mean such love. 95

Lady G. Why, then you mean not as I thought you did.

King Edw. But now you partly may perceive my mind.

Lady G. My mind will never grant what I perceive 100
Your Highness aims at, if I aim aright.

King Edw. To tell thee plain, I aim to lie with thee.

Lady G. To tell you plain, I had rather lie in prison.

King Edw. Why, then thou shalt not have thy husband's lands. 105

Lady G. Why, then mine honesty shall be my dower;
For by that loss I will not purchase them.

114. **sadness:** gravity.
126. **challenge sovereignty:** claim royalty.
139. **mean:** lowly born.

King Edw. Therein thou wrongst thy children mightily. 110

Lady G. Herein your Highness wrongs both them and me.
But, mighty lord, this merry inclination
Accords not with the sadness of my suit.
Please you dismiss me, either with "ay" or "no." 115

King Edw. Ay, if thou wilt say "ay" to my request;
No, if thou dost say "no" to my demand.

Lady G. Then, no, my lord. My suit is at an end.

Glou. [*Aside to Clarence*] The widow likes him not, she knits her brows. 120

Clar. [*Aside to Gloucester*] He is the bluntest wooer in Christendom.

King Edw. [*Aside*] Her looks doth argue her replete with modesty;
Her words doth show her wit incomparable; 125
All her perfections challenge sovereignty.
One way or other, she is for a king;
And she shall be my love, or else my queen.—
Say that King Edward take thee for his queen?

Lady G. 'Tis better said than done, my gracious lord: 130
I am a subject fit to jest withal
But far unfit to be a sovereign.

King Edw. Sweet widow, by my state I swear to thee, 135
I speak no more than what my soul intends;
And that is, to enjoy thee for my love.

Lady G. And that is more than I will yield unto.
I know I am too mean to be your queen,

149. **happy:** fortunate.

152. **ghostly father:** priest.

153. **done his shrift:** heard the confession.

155. **for shift:** a matter of trickery.

156. **muse:** wonder.

158. **sad:** grave.

163. **ten days' wonder:** it was proverbially said that "A wonder lasts but nine days."

165. **in extremes:** extraordinary in character.

And yet too good to be your concubine. 140

King Edw. You cavil, widow: I did mean, my queen.

Lady G. 'Twill grieve your Grace my sons should call you father.

King Edw. No more than when my daughters call thee mother. 145
Thou art a widow and thou hast some children;
And, by God's mother, I, being but a bachelor,
Have othersome: why, 'tis a happy thing
To be the father unto many sons. 150
Answer no more, for thou shalt be my queen.

Glou. [*Aside to Clarence*] The ghostly father now hath done his shrift.

Clar. [*Aside to Gloucester*] When he was made a shriver, 'twas for shift. 155

King Edw. Brothers, you muse what chat we two have had.

Glou. The widow likes it not, for she looks very sad.

King Edw. You'ld think it strange if I should marry her. 160

Clar. To who, my lord?

King Edw. Why, Clarence, to myself.

Glou. That would be ten days' wonder at the least.

Clar. That's a day longer than a wonder lasts.

Glou. By so much is the wonder in extremes. 165

King Edw. Well, jest on, brothers: I can tell you both,
Her suit is granted for her husband's lands.

Enter a Nobleman.

183. **unlooked-for:** unsought, or undesired (by Richard).

184. **rooms:** places.

185. **cold premeditation:** comfortless prospect.

191. **lade:** bale.

196. **quick:** lively; **o'erweens:** presumes.

Gloucester as Richard III. From a manuscript commonplace book by Thomas Trevelyan (*ca.* 1608).

Noble. My gracious lord, Henry your foe is taken,
And brought your prisoner to your palace gate. 170
King Edw. See that he be conveyed unto the
Tower:
And go we, brothers, to the man that took him,
To question of his apprehension.
Widow, go you along. Lords, use her honorably. 175
Exeunt. Manet Gloucester.
Glou. Ay, Edward will use women honorably.
Would he were wasted, marrow, bones, and all,
That from his loins no hopeful branch may spring
To cross me from the golden time I look for!
And yet, between my soul's desire and me— 180
The lustful Edward's title buried—
Is Clarence, Henry, and his son young Edward,
And all the unlooked-for issue of their bodies
To take their rooms, ere I can place myself.
A cold premeditation for my purpose! 185
Why, then, I do but dream on sovereignty
Like one that stands upon a promontory
And spies a far-off shore where he would tread,
Wishing his foot were equal with his eye,
And chides the sea that sunders him from thence, 190
Saying he'll lade it dry to have his way:
So do I wish the crown, being so far off;
And so I chide the means that keeps me from it;
And so I say I'll cut the causes off,
Flattering me with impossibilities. 195
My eye's too quick, my heart o'erweens too much,
Unless my hand and strength could equal them.
Well, say there is no kingdom then for Richard,

202. **witch:** bewitch.

204. **accomplish:** gain.

209. **envious:** hateful.

213. **unlicked bear whelp:** it was believed that bear cubs were born shapeless masses that were licked into shape by their mothers.

223. **impaled:** encircled.

225. **home:** my goal.

Sinon, looking down on Troy. From Geoffrey Whitney, *A Choice of Emblems* (1586). (See III. ii. 242.)

What other pleasure can the world afford?
I'll make my Heaven in a lady's lap, 200
And deck my body in gay ornaments,
And witch sweet ladies with my words and looks.
O miserable thought! and more unlikely
Than to accomplish twenty golden crowns!
Why, love forswore me in my mother's womb; 205
And, for I should not deal in her soft laws,
She did corrupt frail nature with some bribe,
To shrink mine arm up like a withered shrub;
To make an envious mountain on my back,
Where sits deformity to mock my body; 210
To shape my legs of an unequal size;
To disproportion me in every part,
Like to a chaos, or an unlicked bear whelp
That carries no impression like the dam.
And am I then a man to be beloved? 215
O monstrous fault, to harbor such a thought!
Then, since this earth affords no joy to me
But to command, to check, to o'erbear such
As are of better person than myself,
I'll make my Heaven to dream upon the crown, 220
And, whiles I live, t' account this world but hell
Until my misshaped trunk that bears this head
Be round impaled with a glorious crown.
And yet I know not how to get the crown,
For many lives stand between me and home: 225
And I—like one lost in a thorny wood,
That rents the thorns and is rent with the thorns,
Seeking a way and straying from the way;
Not knowing how to find the open air,

238. **mermaid:** i.e., siren, whose singing lured sailors to wreck their vessels on rocks.

239. **basilisk:** a fabulous serpent whose glance was fatal.

240. **Nestor:** King of Pylos, wisest of the Greek leaders described in Homer's *Iliad.*

242. **Sinon:** the Greek Sinon, who allowed himself to be captured by the Trojans, persuaded them to bring in the wooden horse filled with Greek soldiers, who captured Troy.

244. **with:** like; **Proteus:** a sea-god with prophetic powers and the ability to change his shape, which he exercised in order to avoid answering questions about the future.

245. **set . . . Machiavel to school:** instruct Machiavelli in crafty expedience. The *Principe* of Niccolò Machiavelli had earned him a reputation in England as an advocate of the principle that any means is justified to gain one's ends.

[III.iii.] Queen Margaret sues to King Lewis for aid in regaining her husband's throne. The King is sympathetic and courteous to Margaret. However, when Warwick proposes a marriage between King Edward and the King's sister-in-law, Bona of Savoy, he consents, and Margaret's cause seems lost. A messenger brings letters reporting that King Edward has married Lady Grey. King Lewis, enraged, turns upon Warwick, who is so humiliated by Edward's lack of faith that he vows revenge. He and Queen Margaret agree to join together to overthrow Edward and reseat Henry on the throne. Warwick predicts

But toiling desperately to find it out— 230
Torment myself to catch the English crown:
And from that torment I will free myself
Or hew my way out with a bloody ax.
Why, I can smile, and murder whiles I smile,
And cry, "Content" to that which grieves my heart, 235
And wet my cheeks with artificial tears,
And frame my face to all occasions.
I'll drown more sailors than the mermaid shall;
I'll slay more gazers than the basilisk;
I'll play the orator as well as Nestor, 240
Deceive more slyly than Ulysses could,
And, like a Sinon, take another Troy.
I can add colors to the chameleon,
Change shapes with Proteus for advantages,
And set the murderous Machiavel to school. 245
Can I do this and cannot get a crown?
Tut, were it farther off, I'll pluck it down.

Exit.

[Scene III. France. The King's palace.]

Flourish. Enter Lewis the French king; his sister Bona; his Admiral, called Bourbon; Prince Edward; Queen Margaret; and the Earl of Oxford. Lewis sits and riseth up again.

King L. Fair Queen of England, worthy Margaret,
Sit down with us: it ill befits thy state

that Clarence can be won from his allegiance to Edward, and King Lewis promises assistance. It is further agreed that Warwick's daughter shall marry the Prince of Wales.

7. **strike her sail:** humble herself.
9. **Albion:** poetic name for Great Britain.
19. **still:** ever.
31. **of:** from.
32. **forlorn:** forsaken one.

And birth that thou shouldst stand while Lewis doth sit.

Queen M. No, mighty King of France: now Margaret 5
Must strike her sail and learn a while to serve
Where kings command. I was, I must confess,
Great Albion's queen in former golden days:
But now mischance hath trod my title down 10
And with dishonor laid me on the ground,
Where I must take like seat unto my fortune
And to my humble seat conform myself.

King L. Why, say, fair queen, whence springs this deep despair? 15

Queen M. From such a cause as fills mine eyes with tears
And stops my tongue, while heart is drowned in cares.

King L. Whate'er it be, be thou still like thyself
And sit thee by our side. *(Seats her by him.)* Yield not thy neck 20
To fortune's yoke, but let thy dauntless mind
Still ride in triumph over all mischance.
Be plain, Queen Margaret, and tell thy grief:
It shall be eased, if France can yield relief. 25

Queen M. Those gracious words revive my drooping thoughts
And give my tongue-tied sorrows leave to speak.
Now, therefore, be it known to noble Lewis
That Henry, sole possessor of my love, 30
Is of a king become a banished man
And forced to live in Scotland a forlorn;
While proud ambitious Edward Duke of York

38. **crave:** request.

49. **stay:** a pun on another meaning, "support."

50–1. **impatience waiteth on true sorrow:** anxiety inevitably accompanies real sorrow.

Louis XI of France. From Bernardo Giunti, *Cronica breve de i fatti illustri de re di Francia* (1588).

Usurps the regal title and the seat
Of England's true-anointed lawful king. 35
This is the cause that I, poor Margaret,
With this my son, Prince Edward, Henry's heir,
Am come to crave thy just and lawful aid;
And if thou fail us, all our hope is done.
Scotland hath will to help but cannot help; 40
Our people and our peers are both misled,
Our treasure seized, our soldiers put to flight,
And, as thou seest, ourselves in heavy plight.

King L. Renowned queen, with patience calm the storm, 45
While we bethink a means to break it off.

Queen M. The more we stay, the stronger grows our foe.

King L. The more I stay, the more I'll succor thee.

Queen M. Oh, but impatience waiteth on true sorrow. 50
And see where comes the breeder of my sorrow!

Enter Warwick.

King L. What's he approacheth boldly to our presence?

Queen M. Our Earl of Warwick, Edward's greatest friend. 55

King L. Welcome, brave Warwick! What brings thee to France? *He descends. She ariseth.*

Queen M. Ay, now begins a second storm to rise;
For this is he that moves both wind and tide. 60

67. **vouchsafe:** condescend.
68. **sister:** i.e., sister-in-law.
74. **leave and favor:** gracious permission.
85. **purchase:** gain.

War. From worthy Edward, King of Albion,
My lord and sovereign and thy vowed friend,
I come, in kindness and unfeigned love,
First, to do greetings to thy royal person;
And then to crave a league of amity; 65
And lastly to confirm that amity
With nuptial knot, if thou vouchsafe to grant
That virtuous Lady Bona, thy fair sister,
To England's king in lawful marriage.

Queen M. [*Aside*] If that go forward, Henry's hope is done. 70

War. (*Speaking to Bona*) And, gracious madam, in our king's behalf,
I am commanded, with your leave and favor,
Humbly to kiss your hand and with my tongue 75
To tell the passion of my sovereign's heart,
Where fame, late ent'ring at his heedful ears,
Hath placed thy beauty's image and thy virtue.

Queen M. King Lewis and Lady Bona, hear me speak 80
Before you answer Warwick. His demand
Springs not from Edward's well-meant honest love,
But from deceit bred by necessity;
For how can tyrants safely govern home
Unless abroad they purchase great alliance? 85
To prove him tyrant this reason may suffice,
That Henry liveth still; but, were he dead,
Yet here Prince Edward stands, King Henry's son.
Look, therefore, Lewis, that by this league and marriage 90
Thou draw not on thy danger and dishonor;

92. **sway the rule:** maintain power of ruling.

93. **Time suppresseth wrongs:** proverbially, "Time tries all things," and "Truth is the daughter of Time."

94. **Injurious:** insulting.

99. **did subdue the greatest part of Spain:** an exaggeration. Gaunt married as his second wife Constance, daughter of Pedro the Cruel, King of Castile and Léon, and for a time assumed the title King of Castile, but his expeditions to subdue the country had little success.

101. **mirror:** model.

110. **silly:** insignificant.

111. **prescription:** a legal term meaning a claim based on long possession.

115. **bewray:** betray.

116. **fence:** defend.

117. **buckler:** shield.

119. **doom:** sentence.

120. **Aubrey Vere:** executed for treason against Edward's government in 1462.

121. **my father:** executed along with his son.

For though usurpers sway the rule a while,
Yet Heav'ns are just, and Time suppresseth wrongs.
War. Injurious Margaret!
Prince. And why not Queen? 95
War. Because thy father Henry did usurp;
And thou no more art Prince than she is Queen.
Oxf. Then Warwick disannuls great John of Gaunt,
Which did subdue the greatest part of Spain;
And, after John of Gaunt, Henry the Fourth, 100
Whose wisdom was a mirror to the wisest;
And, after that wise prince, Henry the Fifth,
Who by his prowess conquered all France:
From these our Henry lineally descends.
War. Oxford, how haps it, in this smooth discourse, 105
You told not how Henry the Sixth hath lost
All that which Henry the Fifth had gotten?
Methinks these peers of France should smile at that.
But for the rest, you tell a pedigree
Of threescore and two years: a silly time 110
To make prescription for a kingdom's worth.
Oxf. Why, Warwick, canst thou speak against thy liege,
Whom thou obeyedst thirty and six years,
And not bewray thy treason with a blush? 115
War. Can Oxford, that did ever fence the right,
Now buckler falsehood with a pedigree?
For shame! leave Henry, and call Edward king.
Oxf. Call him my king by whose injurious doom
My elder brother, the Lord Aubrey Vere, 120
Was done to death? and more than so, my father,
Even in the downfall of his mellowed years,

133–34. **even upon thy conscience:** truly, from your heart.

138. **gracious:** popular.

149. **Exempt from envy, but not from disdain:** i.e., his love is incapable of changing to dislike, but it is subject to feeling pain if she should disdain it.

150. **quit his pain:** requite his emotion.

When nature brought him to the door of death?
No, Warwick, no; while life upholds this arm,
This arm upholds the house of Lancaster. 125

War. And I the house of York.

King L. Queen Margaret, Prince Edward, and Oxford,
Vouchsafe, at our request, to stand aside,
While I use further conference with Warwick. 130

They stand aloof.

Queen M. Heavens grant that Warwick's words bewitch him not!

King L. Now, Warwick, tell me, even upon thy conscience,
Is Edward your true king? for I were loath 135
To link with him that were not lawful chosen.

War. Thereon I pawn my credit and mine honor.

King L. But is he gracious in the people's eye?

War. The more that Henry was unfortunate.

King L. Then further, all dissembling set aside, 140
Tell me for truth the measure of his love
Unto our sister Bona.

War. Such it seems
As may beseem a monarch like himself.
Myself have often heard him say and swear 145
That this his love was an eternal plant,
Whereof the root was fixed in virtue's ground,
The leaves and fruit maintained with beauty's sun,
Exempt from envy, but not from disdain,
Unless the Lady Bona quit his pain. 150

King L. Now, sister, let us hear your firm resolve.

Bona. Your grant, or your denial, shall be mine:

155. **desert:** merits.
160. **jointure:** marriage settlement.
161. **counterpoised:** balanced.
174. **estate:** state.
177. **quondam:** onetime.

(Speaks to Warwick) Yet I confess that often ere this day,
When I have heard your king's desert recounted, 155
Mine ear hath tempted judgment to desire.

King L. Then, Warwick, thus: our sister shall be Edward's;
And now forthwith shall articles be drawn
Touching the jointure that your king must make, 160
Which with her dowry shall be counterpoised.
Draw near, Queen Margaret, and be a witness
That Bona shall be wife to the English king.

Prince. To Edward, but not to the English king.

Queen M. Deceitful Warwick! it was thy device 165
By this alliance to make void my suit.
Before thy coming Lewis was Henry's friend.

King L. And still is friend to him and Margaret:
But if your title to the crown be weak,
As may appear by Edward's good success, 170
Then 'tis but reason that I be released
From giving aid which late I promised.
Yet shall you have all kindness at my hand
That your estate requires and mine can yield.

War. Henry now lives in Scotland at his ease, 175
Where, having nothing, nothing can he lose.
And as for you yourself, our quondam queen,
You have a father able to maintain you,
And better 'twere you troubled him than France.

Queen M. Peace, impudent and shameless Warwick, peace, 180
Proud setter-up and puller-down of kings!
I will not hence till, with my talk and tears,

185. **conveyance:** artifice; dishonesty.
187. **post:** messenger.
196. **as:** as if.
206. **soothe:** smooth over; **forgery:** falsehood.

Both full of truth, I make King Lewis behold
Thy sly conveyance and thy lord's false love: 185
For both of you are birds of selfsame feather.

Post blowing a horn within.

King L. Warwick, this is some post to us or thee.

Enter the Post.

Post. (*To Warwick*) My lord ambassador, these letters are for you,
Sent from your brother, Marquess Montagu: 190
(*To Lewis*) These from our king unto your Majesty:
(*To Margaret*) And, madam, these for you; from whom, I know not. *They all read their letters.*

Oxf. I like it well that our fair queen and mistress
Smiles at her news, while Warwick frowns at his 195

Prince. Nay, mark how Lewis stamps, as he were nettled.
I hope all's for the best.

King L. Warwick, what are thy news? And yours, fair queen? 200

Queen M. Mine, such as fill my heart with unhoped joys.

War. Mine, full of sorrow and heart's discontent.

King L. What! has your king married the Lady Grey? 205
And now, to soothe your forgery and his,
Sends me a paper to persuade me patience?
Is this the alliance that he seeks with France?
Dare he presume to scorn us in this manner?

217. **by the house of York:** i.e., because of his support of the Yorkists; Salisbury had been executed after the Battle of Wakefield.

219. **the abuse done to my niece:** the exact details are unknown, but Edward tried to seduce one of Warwick's female relatives.

220. **impale:** encircle.

222. **guerdoned:** rewarded.

236. **chosen:** select; choice.

Queen M. I told your Majesty as much before: 210
This proveth Edward's love and Warwick's honesty.
War. King Lewis, I here protest, in sight of Heaven,
And by the hope I have of heavenly bliss,
That I am clear from this misdeed of Edward's,
No more my king, for he dishonors me, 215
But most himself, if he could see his shame.
Did I forget that by the house of York
My father came untimely to his death?
Did I let pass the abuse done to my niece?
Did I impale him with the regal crown? 220
Did I put Henry from his native right?
And am I guerdoned at the last with shame?
Shame on himself! for my desert is honor:
And, to repair my honor lost for him,
I here renounce him and return to Henry. 225
My noble queen, let former grudges pass,
And henceforth I am thy true servitor.
I will revenge his wrong to Lady Bona,
And replant Henry in his former state.
Queen M. Warwick, these words have turned my hate to love; 230
And I forgive and quite forget old faults
And joy that thou becomest King Henry's friend.
War. So much his friend, ay, his unfeigned friend,
That, if King Lewis vouchsafe to furnish us 235
With some few bands of chosen soldiers,
I'll undertake to land them on our coast
And force the tyrant from his seat by war.
'Tis not his new-made bride shall succor him.
And as for Clarence, as my letters tell me, 240

241. **fall from him:** fall away from him; desert him.

261. **fear:** frighten.

264. **the willow garland:** a symbol of unrequited love.

265. **weeds:** garments.

He's very likely now to fall from him,
For matching more for wanton lust than honor
Or than for strength and safety of our country.
Bona. Dear brother, how shall Bona be revenged
But by thy help to this distressed queen? 245
Queen M. Renowned prince, how shall poor Henry live,
Unless thou rescue him from foul despair?
Bona. My quarrel and this English queen's are one.
War. And mine, fair Lady Bona, joins with yours. 250
King L. And mine with hers, and thine, and Margaret's.
Therefore at last I firmly am resolved
You shall have aid.
Queen M. Let me give humble thanks for all at once. 255
King L. Then, England's messenger, return in post
And tell false Edward, thy supposed king,
That Lewis of France is sending over masquers
To revel it with him and his new bride. 260
Thou seest what's passed, go fear thy king withal.
Bona. Tell him, in hope he'll prove a widower shortly,
I wear the willow garland for his sake.
Queen M. Tell him, my mourning weeds are laid aside, 265
And I am ready to put armor on.
War. Tell him from me that he hath done me wrong,
And therefore I'll uncrown him ere't be long. 270
There's thy reward: be gone. *Exit Post.*

275. **occasion:** opportunity.

281. **eldest daughter:** actually, young Edward married Anne Neville, Warwick's youngest daughter, while George, Duke of Clarence, later married Isabella, the eldest.

284. **motion:** offer.

296. **mocking:** making only a pretense of.

299. **charge:** commission.

King L. But, Warwick,
Thou and Oxford, with five thousand men,
Shall cross the seas and bid false Edward battle;
And, as occasion serves, this noble queen 275
And prince shall follow with a fresh supply.
Yet, ere thou go, but answer me one doubt,
What pledge have we of thy firm loyalty?
War. This shall assure my constant loyalty,
That if our queen and this young prince agree, 280
I'll join mine eldest daughter and my joy
To him forthwith in holy wedlock bands.
Queen M. Yes, I agree, and thank you for your motion.
Son Edward, she is fair and virtuous, 285
Therefore delay not, give thy hand to Warwick;
And, with thy hand, thy faith irrevocable
That only Warwick's daughter shall be thine.
Prince. Yes, I accept her, for she well deserves it;
And here, to pledge my vow, I give my hand. 290
He gives his hand to Warwick.
King L. Why stay we now? These soldiers shall be levied,
And thou, Lord Bourbon, our high admiral,
Shall waft them over with our royal fleet.
I long till Edward fall by war's mischance 295
For mocking marriage with a dame of France.
Exeunt. Manet Warwick.
War. I came from Edward as ambassador,
But I return his sworn and mortal foe:
Matter of marriage was the charge he gave me,
But dreadful war shall answer his demand. 300

301. **stale:** dupe.

Had he none else to make a stale but me?
Then none but I shall turn his jest to sorrow.
I was the chief that raised him to the crown,
And I'll be chief to bring him down again:
Not that I pity Henry's misery 305
But seek revenge on Edward's mockery.

Exit.

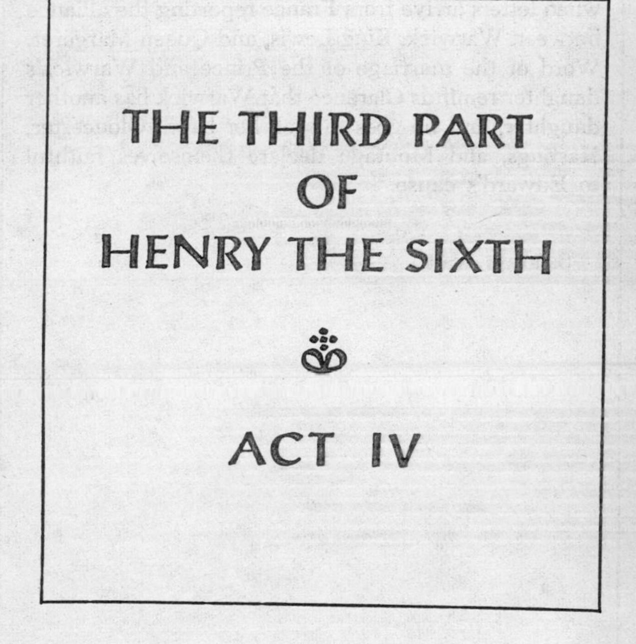
THE THIRD PART
OF
HENRY THE SIXTH
ACT IV

[IV.i.] Richard and George, displeased at their brother's marriage, warn him of the evil that will result, but Edward is complacent. They further reproach him with the favors shown the Queen's family. Edward learns the truth of his brother's foreboding when letters arrive from France reporting the alliance between Warwick, King Lewis, and Queen Margaret. Word of the marriage of the Prince and Warwick's daughter reminds Clarence that Warwick has another daughter, and he goes to seek her hand. Gloucester, Hastings, and Montagu declare themselves faithful to Edward's cause.

6. **stay:** wait.

[*ACT IV*]

[Scene I. London. The palace.]

Enter Gloucester, Clarence, Somerset, and Montagu.

Glou. Now tell me, brother Clarence, what think you
Of this new marriage with the Lady Grey?
Hath not our brother made a worthy choice?
Clar. Alas, you know, 'tis far from hence to France; 5
How could he stay till Warwick made return?
Som. My lords, forbear this talk: here comes the King.
Glou. And his well-chosen bride.
Clar. I mind to tell him plainly what I think. 10

Flourish. Enter King Edward, [*attended;*] *Lady Grey,* [*as Queen Elizabeth*]; *Pembroke, Stafford, Hastings: four stand on one side and four on the other.*

King Edw. Now, brother of Clarence, how like you our choice,
That you stand pensive, as half malcontent?
Clar. As well as Lewis of France or the Earl of Warwick, 15

17. **abuse:** deceit.

Edward IV. From John Speed, *The Theatre of the Empire of Great Britain* (1627).

Which are so weak of courage and in judgment
That they'll take no offense at our abuse.
King Edw. Suppose they take offense without a cause,
They are but Lewis and Warwick: I am Edward, 20
Your king and Warwick's, and must have my will.
Glou. And shall have your will, because our king:
Yet hasty marriage seldom proveth well.
King Edw. Yea, brother Richard, are you offended too? 25
Glou. Not I:
No, God forbid that I should wish them severed
Whom God hath joined together; ay, and 'twere pity
To sunder them that yoke so well together.
King Edw. Setting your scorns and your mislike aside, 30
Tell me some reason why the Lady Grey
Should not become my wife and England's queen.
And you too, Somerset and Montagu,
Speak freely what you think. 35
Clar. Then this is mine opinion: that King Lewis
Becomes your enemy, for mocking him
About the marriage of the Lady Bona.
Glou. And Warwick, doing what you gave in charge, 40
Is now dishonored by this new marriage.
King Edw. What if both Lewis and Warwick be appeased
By such invention as I can devise?
Mon. Yet, to have joined with France in such alliance 45

60. **the heir of the Lord Hungerford:** Mary Hungerford, daughter and heir of Sir Thomas Hungerford, who was executed for supporting Warwick's conspiracy in 1469. Hastings was granted her wardship in 1478 and married her to his son several years later.

66. **the heir and daughter of Lord Scales:** Elizabeth, daughter of Thomas, seventh Baron Scales, was given in marriage to Anthony Woodville, later Earl Rivers and Lord Scales.

69. **in your bride you bury brotherhood:** i.e., his brothers are forgotten in his eagerness to please his bride.

70–1. **the heir/ Of the Lord Bonville:** Cicely Harrington, whose father was William Lord Harrington and Bonville, married Richard Grey, Marquess of Dorset.

72. **speed:** prosper (as best they can).

Would more have strengthened this our common-
wealth
'Gainst foreign storms than any home-bred marriage.
Hast. Why, knows not Montagu that of itself 50
England is safe, if true within itself?
Mont. But the safer when 'tis backed with France.
Hast. 'Tis better using France than trusting France.
Let us be backed with God and with the seas,
Which He hath giv'n for fence impregnable, 55
And with their helps only defend ourselves:
In them and in ourselves our safety lies.
Clar. For this one speech Lord Hastings well de-
serves
To have the heir of the Lord Hungerford. 60
King Edw. Ay, what of that? It was my will and
grant;
And for this once my will shall stand for law.
Glou. And yet methinks your Grace hath not done
well 65
To give the heir and daughter of Lord Scales
Unto the brother of your loving bride:
She better would have fitted me or Clarence;
But in your bride you bury brotherhood.
Clar. Or else you would not have bestowed the heir 70
Of the Lord Bonville on your new wife's son
And leave your brothers to go speed elsewhere.
King Edw. Alas, poor Clarence! is it for a wife
That thou art malcontent? I will provide thee.
Clar. In choosing for yourself, you showed your 75
judgment,

77. **shall give me leave:** must allow me.

85. **descent:** the Queen's mother was the widow of John, Duke of Bedford, brother of Henry V, and daughter of the Luxembourgian Count of St. Pol; Sir Richard Woodville was her second husband.

GEORGE DUKE of CLARENCE.

George, Duke of Clarence. Engraving by Silvester Harding after a drawing in the British Museum.

Which being shallow, you shall give me leave
To play the broker in mine own behalf,
And to that end I shortly mind to leave you.
King Edw. Leave me, or tarry, Edward will be King 80
And not be tied unto his brother's will.
Queen E. My lords, before it pleased His Majesty
To raise my state to title of a queen,
Do me but right and you must all confess
That I was not ignoble of descent; 85
And meaner than myself have had like fortune.
But as this title honors me and mine,
So your dislikes, to whom I would be pleasing,
Doth cloud my joys with danger and with sorrow.
King Edw. My love, forbear to fawn upon their frowns: 90
What danger or what sorrow can befall thee,
So long as Edward is thy constant friend
And their true sovereign, whom they must obey?
Nay, whom they shall obey, and love thee too, 95
Unless they seek for hatred at my hands;
Which if they do, yet will I keep thee safe,
And they shall feel the vengeance of my wrath.
Glou. [*Aside*] I hear, yet say not much, but think the more. 100

Enter a Post.

King Edw. Now, messenger, what letters or what news
From France?
Post. My sovereign liege, no letters; and few words

107. **Go to:** come, come!
115. **brave:** defiant.
128. **minds:** intends.

But such as I, without your special pardon, 105
Dare not relate.

King Edw. Go to! we pardon thee: therefore, in brief,
Tell me their words as near as thou canst guess them.
What answers makes King Lewis unto our letters? 110

Post. At my depart these were his very words:
"Go tell false Edward, thy supposed king,
That Lewis of France is sending over masquers
To revel it with him and his new bride."

King Edw. Is Lewis so brave? Belike he thinks me Henry. 115
But what said Lady Bona to my marriage?

Post. These were her words, uttered with mild disdain:
"Tell him, in hope he'll prove a widower shortly, 120
I'll wear the willow garland for his sake."

King Edw. I blame not her, she could say little less;
She had the wrong. But what said Henry's queen?
For I have heard that she was there in place.

Post. "Tell him," quoth she, "my mourning weeds are done, 125
And I am ready to put armor on."

King Edw. Belike she minds to play the Amazon.
But what said Warwick to these injuries?

Post. He, more incensed against your Majesty 130
Than all the rest, discharged me with these words:
"Tell him from me that he hath done me wrong,
And therefore I'll uncrown him ere't be long."

King Edw. Ha! durst the traitor breathe out so proud words? 135

145. **sit you fast:** make your seat secure against attack.

147. **That:** so that; **want:** lack.

160. **straight:** immediately.

163. **by blood and by alliance:** Montagu was Warwick's brother, thus related **by blood;** Hastings was married to Catherine Neville, Warwick's sister, thus related **by alliance.**

Well, I will arm me, being thus forewarned.
They shall have wars and pay for their presumption.
But say, is Warwick friends with Margaret?

Post. Ay, gracious sovereign; they are so linked in friendship 140
That young Prince Edward marries Warwick's daughter.

Clar. Belike the elder; Clarence will have the younger.
Now, brother king, farewell, and sit you fast, 145
For I will hence to Warwick's other daughter;
That, though I want a kingdom, yet in marriage
I may not prove inferior to yourself.
You that love me and Warwick, follow me.

Exit Clarence, and Somerset follows.

Glou. [*Aside*] Not I. 150
My thoughts aim at a further matter: I
Stay not for the love of Edward but the crown.

King Edw. Clarence and Somerset both gone to Warwick!
Yet am I armed against the worst can happen, 155
And haste is needful in this desp'rate case.
Pembroke and Stafford, you in our behalf
Go levy men and make prepare for war:
They are already, or quickly will be, landed.
Myself in person will straight follow you. 160

Exeunt Pembroke and Stafford.

But, ere I go, Hastings and Montagu,
Resolve my doubt. You twain, of all the rest,
Are near to Warwick by blood and by alliance:
Tell me if you love Warwick more than me.

166. **hollow:** insincere.
169. **suspect:** suspicion.

[IV.ii.] Warwick, who has gained followers since his return to England, is joined by Clarence and Somerset. He reveals his plan to fall upon Edward unawares in his camp and take him prisoner.

If it be so, then both depart to him; 165
I rather wish you foes than hollow friends:
But if you mind to hold your true obedience,
Give me assurance with some friendly vow,
That I may never have you in suspect.

Mon. So God help Montagu as he proves true! 170

Hast. And Hastings as he favors Edward's cause!

King Edw. Now, brother Richard, will you stand by us?

Glou. Ay, in despite of all that shall withstand you.

King Edw. Why, so! then am I sure of victory. 175
Now therefore let us hence and lose no hour,
Till we meet Warwick with his foreign pow'r.

Exeunt.

[Scene II. A plain in Warwickshire.]

Enter Warwick and Oxford, in England, with French soldiers.

War. Trust me, my lord, all hitherto goes well;
The common people by numbers swarm to us.

Enter Clarence and Somerset.

But see where Somerset and Clarence comes!
Speak suddenly, my lords, are we all friends?

Clar. Fear not that, my lord. 5

12. **feigned:** pretended.
15. **rests:** remains; **coverture:** concealment.
18. **simple:** weak; feeble.
21. **stout:** brave.
22. **sleight and manhood:** valiant trickery.
23. **the Thracian fatal steeds:** Rhesus, King of Thrace, brought with him to the siege of Troy some beautiful horses. An oracle had decreed that Troy could never be taken if these steeds drank the water of the Xanthus (Scamander) River, near the city. The theft of the horses by Ulysses and Diomedes prevented fulfillment of the oracle, and Troy ultimately fell.
25. **At unawares:** when they are unaware.
27. **surprise:** capture.
30. **in silent sort:** silently.

War. Then, gentle Clarence, welcome unto Warwick;
And welcome, Somerset. I hold it cowardice
To rest mistrustful where a noble heart
Hath pawned an open hand in sign of love; 10
Else might I think that Clarence, Edward's brother,
Were but a feigned friend to our proceedings:
But welcome, sweet Clarence; my daughter shall be thine.
And now what rests but, in night's coverture, 15
Thy brother being carelessly encamped,
His soldiers lurking in the town about,
And but attended by a simple guard,
We may surprise and take him at our pleasure?
Our scouts have found the adventure very easy: 20
That, as Ulysses and stout Diomede
With sleight and manhood stole to Rhesus' tents
And brought from thence the Thracian fatal steeds,
So we, well covered with the night's black mantle,
At unawares may beat down Edward's guard 25
And seize himself: I say not, slaughter him,
For I intend but only to surprise him.
You that will follow me to this attempt,
Applaud the name of Henry with your leader.

They all cry, "Henry!"

Why, then, let's on our way in silent sort: 30
For Warwick and his friends, God and St. George!

Exeunt.

[IV.iii.] King Edward sleeps in his tent with only three men to guard him. Warwick and his party appear and quickly disperse them. Richard and Hastings escape, but Edward is captured. Warwick informs him that, having formerly created him King of England, he has now come to create him Duke of York. Edward is led out to be placed in the custody of Warwick's brother, the Archbishop of York. Warwick's next move will be to free Henry and restore him to his throne.

---

19. **worship:** dignity; i.e., comfort befitting one's estate; **quietness:** privacy.

21. **he:** the King.

22. **doubted:** feared.

23. **shut up:** cut off.

[Scene III. Edward's camp near Warwick.]

Enter three Watchmen, to guard the King's tent.

1. Watch. Come on, my masters, each man take his stand.
The King by this is set him down to sleep.
2. Watch. What, will he not to bed?
1. Watch. Why, no; for he hath made a solemn vow 5
Never to lie and take his natural rest
Till Warwick or himself be quite suppressed.
2. Watch. Tomorrow then belike shall be the day,
If Warwick be so near as men report.
3. Watch. But say, I pray, what nobleman is that 10
That with the King here resteth in his tent?
1. Watch. 'Tis the Lord Hastings, the King's chiefest friend.
3. Watch. Oh, is it so? But why commands the King
That his chief followers lodge in towns about him, 15
While he himself keeps in the cold field?
2. Watch. 'Tis the more honor, because more dangerous.
3. Watch. Ay, but give me worship and quietness;
I like it better than a dangerous honor. 20
If Warwick knew in what estate he stands,
'Tis to be doubted he would waken him.
1. Watch. Unless our halberds did shut up his passage.

40. **embassade:** embassy.

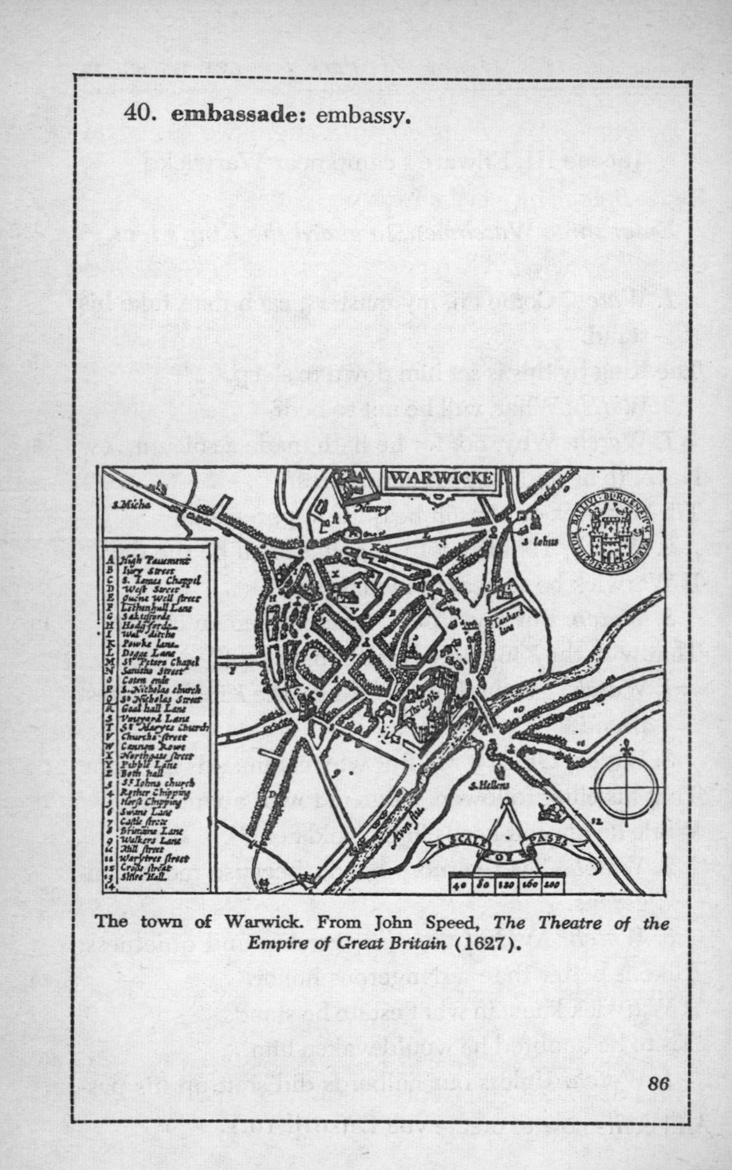

The town of Warwick. From John Speed, *The Theatre of the Empire of Great Britain* (1627).

2. *Watch.* Ay, wherefore else guard we his royal tent, 25
But to defend his person from night foes?

Enter Warwick, Clarence, Oxford, Somerset and French soldiers, silent all.

War. This is his tent; and see where stand his guard.
Courage, my masters! honor now or never!
But follow me, and Edward shall be ours. 30
1. *Watch.* Who goes there?
2. *Watch.* Stay, or thou diest!
Warwick and the rest cry all, "Warwick! Warwick!" and set upon the Guard, who fly, crying, "Arm! arm!" Warwick and the rest following them.

The drum playing and trumpet sounding. Enter Warwick, Somerset, and the rest, bringing the King out in his gown, sitting in a chair. Richard and Hastings fly over the stage.

Som. What are they that fly there?
War. Richard and Hastings. Let them go: here is
The Duke. 35
King Edw. The Duke! Why, Warwick, when we parted,
Thou calledst me King.
War. Ay, but the case is altered.
When you disgraced me in my embassade, 40
Then I degraded you from being King
And come now to create you Duke of York.

47. **study:** plan.

48. **shroud:** shield.

56. **compass:** circuit; sphere of influence; **wheel:** referring to the proverbial wheel by which Fortune was said to control human fate.

57. **for his mind:** so far as Edward's own mind is concerned (but not otherwise).

70. **boots:** avails.

Alas! how should you govern any kingdom
That know not how to use ambassadors,
Nor how to be contented with one wife, 45
Nor how to use your brothers brotherly,
Nor how to study for the people's welfare,
Nor how to shroud yourself from enemies?

King Edw. Yea, brother of Clarence, art thou here too? 50
Nay, then I see that Edward needs must down.
Yet, Warwick, in despite of all mischance,
Of thee thyself and all thy complices,
Edward will always bear himself as King:
Though Fortune's malice overthrow my state, 55
My mind exceeds the compass of her wheel.

War. Then, for his mind, be Edward England's king: *Takes off his crown.*
But Henry now shall wear the English crown
And be true King indeed, thou but the shadow. 60
My lord of Somerset, at my request,
See that forthwith Duke Edward be conveyed
Unto my brother, Archbishop of York.
When I have fought with Pembroke and his fellows,
I'll follow you and tell what answer 65
Lewis and the Lady Bona send to him.
Now, for a while farewell, good Duke of York.

They lead him out forcibly.

King Edw. What Fates impose, that men must needs abide;
It boots not to resist both wind and tide. 70

Exit [*guarded*].

[IV.iv.] Queen Elizabeth, hearing of her husband's capture, resolves to fly to sanctuary, so that no harm will come to the child she is carrying, who should be heir to the crown.

1–2. **makes you in this sudden change:** causes this sudden alteration in you.

4. **late:** recent.

5. **pitched:** formally arrayed.

7. **his own royal person:** i.e., his freedom.

14. **Fell:** deadly.

Oxf. What now remains, my lords, for us to do,
But march to London with our soldiers?
War. Ay, that's the first thing that we have to do;
To free King Henry from imprisonment,
And see him seated in the regal throne. 75
Exeunt.

[Scene IV. London. The palace.]

Enter Queen Elizabeth and Rivers.

Riv. Madam, what makes you in this sudden change?
Queen E. Why, brother Rivers, are you yet to learn
What late misfortune is befall'n King Edward?
Riv. What! loss of some pitched battle against Warwick? 5
Queen E. No, but the loss of his own royal person.
Riv. Then is my sovereign slain?
Queen E. Ay, almost slain, for he is taken prisoner,
Either betrayed by falsehood of his guard, 10
Or by his foe surprised at unawares:
And, as I further have to understand,
Is new committed to the Bishop of York,
Fell Warwick's brother and by that our foe.
Riv. These news I must confess are full of grief; 15
Yet, gracious madam, bear it as you may:
Warwick may lose that now hath won the day.
Queen E. Till then fair hope must hinder life's decay:

22. **passion:** violent grief.

25. **bloodsucking sighs:** sighs were believed to drain blood from the heart.

28. **where is Warwick then become:** what has then become of Warwick.

[IV.v.] Gloucester, with Hastings and others, rescues Edward, who has been allowed to hunt with only one attendant.

And I the rather wean me from despair 20
For love of Edward's offspring in my womb:
This is it that makes me bridle passion
And bear with mildness my misfortune's cross.
Ay, ay, for this I draw in many a tear
And stop the rising of bloodsucking sighs, 25
Lest with my sighs or tears I blast or drown
King Edward's fruit, true heir to the English crown.

Riv. But, madam, where is Warwick then become?

Queen E. I am informed that he comes toward London 30
To set the crown once more on Henry's head.
Guess thou the rest: King Edward's friends must down,
But, to prevent the tyrant's violence—
For trust not him that hath once broken faith— 35
I'll hence forthwith unto the sanctuary,
To save at least the heir of Edward's right.
There shall I rest secure from force and fraud.
Come, therefore, let us fly while we may fly.
If Warwick take us we are sure to die. 40

Exeunt.

[Scene V. A park near Middleham Castle in Yorkshire.]

Enter Gloucester, Lord Hastings, Sir William Stanley [*and others*].

Glou. Now, my Lord Hastings and Sir William Stanley,

3. **Leave off:** cease.

10. **advertised:** informed.

12. **color:** pretext; **game:** sport.

21. **close:** concealed.

28. **meaning:** intention.

29. **requite:** reward; **forwardness:** readiness to be of aid.

Leave off to wonder why I drew you hither
Into this chiefest thicket of the park.
Thus stands the case: you know our king, my brother, 5
Is prisoner to the Bishop here, at whose hands
He hath good usage and great liberty,
And often, but attended with weak guard,
Comes hunting this way to disport himself.
I have advertised him by secret means 10
That if about this hour he make this way,
Under the color of his usual game,
He shall here find his friends with horse and men
To set him free from his captivity.

Enter King Edward and a Huntsman with him.

Hunts. This way, my lord; for this way lies the game. 15

King Edw. Nay, this way, man: see where the huntsmen stand.
Now, brother of Gloucester, Lord Hastings, and the rest, 20
Stand you thus close to steal the Bishop's deer?

Glou. Brother, the time and case requireth haste:
Your horse stands ready at the park corner.

King Edw. But whither shall we then?

Hast. To Lynn, my lord, 25
And ship from thence to Flanders.

Glou. Well guessed, believe me; for that was my meaning.

King Edw. Stanley, I will requite thy forwardness.

Glou. But wherefore stay we? 'Tis no time to talk. 30

[IV.vi.] Warwick releases King Henry from imprisonment in the Tower of London. The King declares his resolve to lead a retired life while Warwick actually governs the realm, and he further names Clarence as Protector. Warwick intends to name Edward a traitor and confiscate his lands. He promises that Clarence will not be forgotten in settling the succession. Henry begs that his wife and son be recalled from France. He notices a youth, identified as Henry, Earl of Richmond, and prophesies that he will in time rule over a happier country than the England which they now know. Word comes of Edward's escape to Burgundy to seek aid for another attempt at the throne. Somerset and Oxford decide to send young Richmond to Brittany for safety.

6. **enlargement:** release; **due fees:** prisoners were charged for their keep.
7. **challenge:** claim.
10. **crave:** request.
13. **For that:** because.

King Edw. Huntsman, what sayst thou? Wilt thou go along?

Hunts. Better do so than tarry and be hanged.

Glou. Come then; away; let's ha' no more ado.

King Edw. Bishop, farewell: shield thee from Warwick's frown; 35

And pray that I may repossess the crown.

Exeunt.

[Scene VI. London. The Tower.]

Flourish. Enter King Henry the Sixth, Clarence, Warwick, Somerset, young Richmond, Oxford, Montagu, and Lieutenant [*of the Tower*].

King H. Master Lieutenant, now that God and friends

Have shaken Edward from the regal seat

And turned my captive state to liberty,

My fear to hope, my sorrows unto joys, 5

At our enlargement what are thy due fees?

Lieut. Subjects may challenge nothing of their sov'reigns;

But if an humble prayer may prevail,

I then crave pardon of your Majesty. 10

King H. For what, Lieutenant? for well using me?

Nay, be thou sure I'll well requite thy kindness,

For that it made my imprisonment a pleasure;

Ay, such a pleasure as incaged birds

Conceive when after many moody thoughts 15

22. **low:** humbly.
24. **thwarting:** adverse.
28. **still:** always.
31. **temper:** come to terms.
33. **in place:** here.
34. **sway:** rule.

At last, by notes of household harmony,
They quite forget their loss of liberty.
But, Warwick, after God, thou setst me free,
And chiefly therefore I thank God and thee:
He was the author, thou the instrument. 20
Therefore, that I may conquer Fortune's spite
By living low, where Fortune cannot hurt me,
And that the people of this blessed land
May not be punished with my thwarting stars,
Warwick, although my head still wear the crown, 25
I here resign my government to thee,
For thou art fortunate in all thy deeds.

War. Your Grace hath still been famed for virtuous;
And now may seem as wise as virtuous
By spying and avoiding Fortune's malice, 30
For few men rightly temper with the stars.
Yet in this one thing let me blame your Grace,
For choosing me when Clarence is in place.

Clar. No, Warwick, thou art worthy of the sway,
To whom the Heav'ns in thy nativity 35
Adjudged an olive branch and laurel crown,
As likely to be blest in peace and war;
And therefore I yield thee my free consent.

War. And I choose Clarence only for Protector.

King H. Warwick and Clarence, give me both your hands: 40
Now join your hands, and with your hands your hearts,
That no dissension hinder government.
I make you both Protectors of this land, 45
While I myself will lead a private life

51. **repose myself:** confidently place myself.

54. **yoke:** work, like a team of draught animals.

55. **supply:** fill.

72–3. **Henry, Earl of Richmond:** the future Henry VII.

Henry, Earl of Richmond (later Henry VII). Engraving by Silvester Harding after Jan de Mabuse.

And in devotion spend my latter days,
To sin's rebuke and my Creator's praise.
War. What answers Clarence to his sovereign's will?
Clar. That he consents, if Warwick yield consent; 50
For on thy fortune I repose myself.
War. Why, then, though loath, yet must I be content.
We'll yoke together, like a double shadow
To Henry's body, and supply his place; 55
I mean, in bearing weight of government,
While he enjoys the honor and his ease.
And, Clarence, now then it is more than needful
Forthwith that Edward be pronounced a traitor
And all his lands and goods be confiscate. 60
Clar. What else? and that succession be determined.
War. Ay, therein Clarence shall not want his part.
King H. But, with the first of all your chief affairs,
Let me entreat, for I command no more,
That Margaret your queen and my son Edward 65
Be sent for, to return from France with speed;
For, till I see them here, by doubtful fear
My joy of liberty is half eclipsed.
Clar. It shall be done, my sovereign, with all speed.
King H. My lord of Somerset, what youth is that 70
Of whom you seem to have so tender care?
Som. My liege, it is young Henry, Earl of Richmond.
King H. Come hither, England's hope. (*Lays his hand on his head.*) If secret powers 75
Suggest but truth to my divining thoughts,
This pretty lad will prove our country's bliss.

Charles, Duke of Burgundy. From Pompilio Totti, *Ritratti et elogii di capitani illustri* (1635).

His looks are full of peaceful majesty,
His head by nature framed to wear a crown,
His hand to wield a scepter, and himself 80
Likely in time to bless a regal throne.
Make much of him, my lords, for this is he
Must help you more than you are hurt by me.

Enter a Post.

War. What news, my friend?
Post. That Edward is escaped from your brother 85
And fled, as he hears since, to Burgundy.
War. Unsavory news! but how made he escape?
Post. He was conveyed by Richard Duke of Gloucester
And the Lord Hastings, who attended him 90
In secret ambush on the forest side
And from the Bishop's huntsmen rescued him;
For hunting was his daily exercise.
War. My brother was too careless of his charge.
But let us hence, my sovereign, to provide 95
A salve for any sore that may betide.
Exeunt. Manent Somerset, Richmond, and Oxford.
Som. My lord, I like not of this flight of Edward's;
For doubtless Burgundy will yield him help
And we shall have more wars before't be long.
As Henry's late presaging prophecy 100
Did glad my heart with hope of this young Richmond,
So doth my heart misgive me, in these conflicts,
What may befall him to his harm and ours.
Therefore, Lord Oxford, to prevent the worst,

108. **like:** likely.

[IV.vii.] Edward and his party arrive at the gates of York and are given the keys. Edward denies that he seeks anything except his rights to the duchy of York. When Sir John Montgomery with a company of men disdains to aid Edward as a mere duke, Edward has himself proclaimed King Edward the Fourth.

---

7. **help from Burgundy:** Edward's sister Margaret had married Charles the Bold, Duke of Burgundy, in 1469.

9. **Ravenspurgh:** consciously or not, Edward followed the pattern of Henry IV's behavior when he returned from exile, both in landing at Ravenspurgh and in claiming only his duchy to begin with.

12–3. **men that stumble at the threshold/ Are well foretold that danger lurks within:** according to popular superstition, such falls boded ill luck.

Forthwith we'll send him hence to Brittany, 105
Till storms be past of civil enmity.
Oxf. Ay, for if Edward repossess the crown,
'Tis like that Richmond with the rest shall down.
Som. It shall be so; he shall to Brittany.
Come, therefore, let's about it speedily. 110
Exeunt.

[Scene VII. Before York.]

Flourish. Enter King Edward, Gloucester, Hastings, and Soldiers.

King Edw. Now, brother Richard, Lord Hastings, and the rest,
Yet thus far Fortune maketh us amends
And says that once more I shall interchange
My waned state for Henry's regal crown. 5
Well have we passed and now repassed the seas
And brought desired help from Burgundy.
What then remains, we being thus arrived
From Ravenspurgh haven before the gates of York,
But that we enter, as into our dukedom? 10
Glou. The gates made fast! Brother, I like not this;
For many men that stumble at the threshold
Are well foretold that danger lurks within.
King Edw. Tush, man, abodements must not now affright us. 15
By fair or foul means we must enter in,

27. **challenge:** claim.

39–40. **would fain that all were well:** i.e., would be glad to see Edward restored to his former state.

41. **So 'twere not long of him:** so long as he was not answerable to the Lancastrian party for the consequences.

For hither will our friends repair to us.

Hast. My liege, I'll knock once more to summon them.

Enter, on the walls, the Mayor of York and his Brethren.

May. My lords, we were forewarnèd of your coming 20
And shut the gates for safety of ourselves;
For now we owe allegiance unto Henry.

King Edw. But, Master Mayor, if Henry be your king,
Yet Edward at the least is Duke of York. 25

May. True, my good lord; I know you for no less.

King Edw. Why, and I challenge nothing but my dukedom,
As being well content with that alone.

Glou. [*Aside*] But when the fox hath once got in his nose, 30
He'll soon find means to make the body follow.

Hast. Why, Master Mayor, why stand you in a doubt?
Open the gates: we are King Henry's friends. 35

May. Ay, say you so? The gates shall then be opened. *They descend.*

Glou. A wise stout captain and soon persuaded!

Hast. The good old man would fain that all were well, 40
So 'twere not long of him; but, being entered,
I doubt not, I, but we shall soon persuade
Both him and all his brothers unto reason.

50. **Sir John:** in Holinshed, Montgomery's first name is Thomas.

61. **I came to serve a king and not a duke:** history records Montgomery as actually saying this.

Enter the Mayor and two Aldermen [below].

King Edw. So, Master Mayor: these gates must not
be shut 45
But in the night or in the time of war.
What! fear not, man, but yield me up the keys,
Takes his keys.
For Edward will defend the town and thee
And all those friends that deign to follow me.

March. Enter Montgomery, with Drum and Soldiers.

Glou. Brother, this is Sir John Montgomery, 50
Our trusty friend, unless I be deceived.
King Edw. Welcome, Sir John! But why come you
in arms?
Mont. To help King Edward in his time of storm,
As every loyal subject ought to do. 55
King Edw. Thanks, good Montgomery; but we now
forget
Our title to the crown and only claim
Our dukedom till God please to send the rest.
Mont. Then fare you well, for I will hence again: 60
I came to serve a king and not a duke.
Drummer, strike up and let us march away.
The Drum begins to march.
King Edw. Nay, stay, Sir John, awhile, and we'll
debate
By what safe means the crown may be recovered. 65

70. **title:** claim.

71–2. **stand . . . on nice points:** hesitate over scruples.

81. **bruit:** rumor.

Mont. What talk you of debating? In few words,
If you'll not here proclaim yourself our king,
I'll leave you to your fortune and be gone
To keep them back that come to succor you.
Why shall we fight if you pretend no title? 70

Glou. Why, brother, wherefore stand you on nice points?

King Edw. When we grow stronger, then we'll make our claim:
Till then, 'tis wisdom to conceal our meaning. 75

Hast. Away with scrupulous wit! now arms must rule.

Glou. And fearless minds climb soonest unto crowns.
Brother, we will proclaim you out of hand: 80
The bruit thereof will bring you many friends.

King Edw. Then be it as you will, for 'tis my right,
And Henry but usurps the diadem.

Mont. Ay, now my sovereign speaketh like himself;
And now will I be Edward's champion. 85

Hast. Sound trumpet: Edward shall be here proclaimed.
Come, fellow soldier, make thou proclamation.

Flourish. Sound.

Sol. Edward the Fourth, by the grace of God, King
of England and France, and Lord of Ireland, etc. 90

Mont. And whosoe'er gainsays King Edward's right,
By this I challenge him to single fight.

Throws down his gauntlet.

All. Long live Edward the Fourth!

101. **wot:** know.
102. **froward:** perverse; **beseems:** becomes.
103. **flatter:** encourage.

[**IV.viii.**] Warwick announces to Henry that Edward has returned from the Low Countries and is marching on London. He orders preparations to answer the threat and suggests that the King stay in London until they return. Clarence vows his fidelity to Henry. Although Henry is hopeful that his virtuous rule will keep his subjects loyal, he has no sooner voiced the thought than Edward and his followers burst in and bear him off to prison in the Tower. Edward orders an immediate departure for Coventry, to surprise Warwick.

2. **hasty:** irritable; **blunt:** rough.

The morning sun in his car. From Claude Menestrier, *L'art des emblemes* (1684).

King Edw. Thanks, brave Montgomery; and thanks unto you all. 95
If fortune serve me, I'll requite this kindness.
Now, for this night, let's harbor here in York;
And when the morning sun shall raise his car
Above the border of this horizon,
We'll forward toward Warwick and his mates; 100
For well I wot that Henry is no soldier.
Ah, froward Clarence! how evil it beseems thee
To flatter Henry and forsake thy brother!
Yet, as we may, we'll meet both thee and Warwick.
Come on, brave soldiers: doubt not of the day, 105
And, that once gotten, doubt not of large pay.

Exeunt.

[Scene VIII. London. The Bishop's palace.]

Flourish. Enter King Henry, Warwick, Montagu, Clarence, [*Exeter*], *and Oxford.*

War. What counsel, lords? Edward from Belgia,
With hasty Germans and blunt Hollanders,
Hath passed in safety through the Narrow Seas
And with his troops doth march amain to London;
And many giddy people flock to him. 5
King H. Let's levy men and beat him back again.
Clar. A little fire is quickly trodden out,
Which, being suffered, rivers cannot quench.
War. In Warwickshire I have true-hearted friends,

21. **Dian:** Diana, the chaste goddess of the hunt.
27. **truth:** loyalty.
32. **at once:** together.
37. **encounter:** match.
38. **doubt:** fear.

Not mutinous in peace, yet bold in war: 10
Those will I muster up. And thou, son Clarence,
Shalt stir up in Suffolk, Norfolk, and in Kent
The knights and gentlemen to come with thee.
Thou, brother Montagu, in Buckingham,
Northampton, and in Leicestershire shalt find 15
Men well inclined to hear what thou commandst.
And thou, brave Oxford, wondrous well beloved,
In Oxfordshire shalt muster up thy friends.
My sovereign, with the loving citizens,
Like to his island girt in with the ocean, 20
Or modest Dian circled with her nymphs,
Shall rest in London till we come to him.
Fair lords, take leave and stand not to reply.
Farewell, my sovereign.

King H. Farewell, my Hector, and my Troy's true hope. 25

Clar. In sign of truth, I kiss your Highness' hand.

King H. Well-minded Clarence, be thou fortunate!

Mon. Comfort, my lord; and so I take my leave.

Oxf. And thus I seal my truth and bid adieu. 30

King H. Sweet Oxford, and my loving Montagu,
And all at once, once more a happy farewell.

War. Farewell, sweet lords: let's meet at Coventry.

Exeunt [*all but King Henry and Exeter*].

King H. Here at the palace will I rest awhile.
Cousin of Exeter, what thinks your Lordship? 35
Methinks the power that Edward hath in field
Should not be able to encounter mine.

Exe. The doubt is that he will seduce the rest.

39. **meed:** merit.
42. **posted off:** put off.
48. **forward of:** prompt to.
50. **graces:** virtues; **grace:** favor.
54. **shamefaced:** bashful; timid.
56. **us:** the royal plural.

King H. That's not my fear: my meed hath got me fame. 40
I have not stopped mine ears to their demands,
Nor posted off their suits with slow delays.
My pity hath been balm to heal their wounds,
My mildness hath allayed their swelling griefs,
My mercy dried their water-flowing tears. 45
I have not been desirous of their wealth
Nor much oppressed them with great subsidies,
Nor forward of revenge, though they much erred:
Then why should they love Edward more than me?
No, Exeter, these graces challenge grace: 50
And when the lion fawns upon the lamb,
The lamb will never cease to follow him.

Shout within, "A Lancaster! A Lancaster!"

Exe. Hark, hark, my lord! what shouts are these?

Enter [King] Edward, [Gloucester,] and Soldiers.

King Edw. Seize on the shamefaced Henry, bear him hence, 55
And once again proclaim us King of England.
You are the fount that makes small brooks to flow:
Now stops thy spring; my sea shall suck them dry
And swell so much the higher by their ebb.
Hence with him to the Tower: let him not speak. 60

Exeunt [some] with King Henry.

And, lords, toward Coventry bend we our course,
Where peremptory Warwick now remains.
The sun shines hot; and, if we use delay,
Cold biting winter mars our hoped-for hay.

Glou. Away betimes, before his forces join, 65
And take the great-grown traitor unawares.
Brave warriors, march amain toward Coventry.

Exeunt.

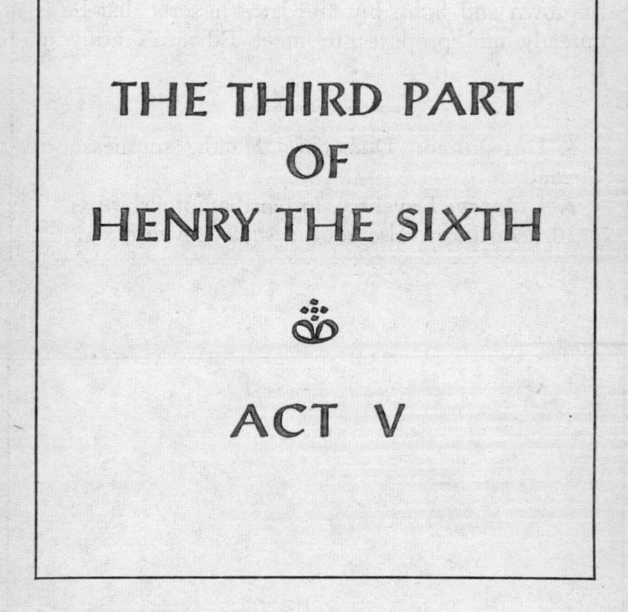

THE THIRD PART OF HENRY THE SIXTH

ACT V

[**V.i.**] Warwick awaits his own allies at Coventry. Edward's arrival, and his news that Henry is a prisoner, take Warwick by surprise. Oxford, Montagu, and Somerset join Warwick in the city, but when Clarence arrives, he defies Warwick and declares for his brother. Edward challenges Warwick to leave the town and fight, but the latter asserts that he is unready and proposes to meet Edward's army at Barnet.

4. **Dunsmore:** Dunsmore Heath, southeast of Coventry.

7. **Daintry:** Daventry, in Northamptonshire.

10. **Southam:** also southeast of Coventry.

[*ACT V*]

[Scene I. Coventry.]

Enter Warwick, the Mayor of Coventry, two Messengers, and others upon the walls.

War. Where is the post that came from valiant Oxford?
How far hence is thy lord, mine honest fellow?
1. Mess. By this at Dunsmore, marching hitherward.
War. How far off is our brother Montagu? 5
Where is the post that came from Montagu?
2. Mess. By this at Daintry, with a puissant troop.

Enter [Sir John] Somerville.

War. Say, Somerville, what says my loving son?
And, by thy guess, how nigh is Clarence now?
Somer. At Southam I did leave him with his forces, 10
And do expect him here some two hours hence.
[*Drum heard.*]
War. Then Clarence is at hand: I hear his drum.
Somer. It is not his, my lord: here Southam lies.
The drum your Honor hears marcheth from Warwick.

22. **sportful:** wanton.

24. **repair:** coming.

36. **make the jest against his will:** i.e., did he say **Duke of York** by a slip of the tongue.

38. **for a poor earl:** dukes rank higher in the peerage than do earls.

39. **service:** i.e., like that of a follower to his feudal lord.

War. Who should that be? Belike, unlooked-for friends. 15

Somer. They are at hand, and you shall quickly know.

March. Flourish. Enter King Edward, Gloucester, and Soldiers.

King Edw. Go, trumpet, to the walls, and sound a parle. 20

Glou. See how the surly Warwick mans the wall!

War. O unbid spite! is sportful Edward come?
Where slept our scouts, or how are they seduced,
That we could hear no news of his repair?

King Edw. Now, Warwick, wilt thou ope the city gates, 25
Speak gentle words, and humbly bend thy knee,
Call Edward king and at his hands beg mercy?
And he shall pardon thee these outrages.

War. Nay, rather, wilt thou draw thy forces hence, 30
Confess who set thee up and plucked thee down,
Call Warwick patron and be penitent?
And thou shalt still remain the Duke of York.

Glou. I thought at least he would have said the King; 35
Or did he make the jest against his will?

War. Is not a dukedom, sir, a goodly gift?

Glou. Ay, by my faith, for a poor earl to give:
I'll do thee service for so good a gift.

War. 'Twas I that gave the kingdom to thy brother. 40

50. **forecast:** foresight.
56. **time:** opportunity.
67. **Wind-changing:** changeable as the wind.

Atlas, with the world on his shoulders. From Gabriele Simeoni, *Le sententiose imprese* (1560).

King Edw. Why then 'tis mine, if but by Warwick's gift.

War. Thou art no Atlas for so great a weight.
And, weakling, Warwick takes his gift again;
And Henry is my king, Warwick his subject. 45

King Edw. But Warwick's king is Edward's prisoner.
And, gallant Warwick, do but answer this:
What is the body when the head is off?

Glou. Alas, that Warwick had no more forecast 50
But, whiles he thought to steal the single ten,
The King was slyly fingered from the deck!
You left poor Henry at the Bishop's palace,
And, ten to one, you'll meet him in the Tower.

King Edw. 'Tis even so: yet you are Warwick still. 55

Glou. Come, Warwick, take the time: kneel down, kneel down.
Nay, when? Strike now, or else the iron cools.

War. I had rather chop this hand off at a blow
And with the other fling it at thy face 60
Than bear so low a sail, to strike to thee.

King Edw. Sail how thou canst, have wind and tide thy friend,
This hand, fast wound about thy coal-black hair,
Shall, whiles thy head is warm and new cut off, 65
Write in the dust this sentence with thy blood,
"Wind-changing Warwick now can change no more."

Enter Oxford, with Drum and Colors.

War. O cheerful colors! see where Oxford comes!

74. **but of small defense:** capable of but slight defense.

85. **two of thy name:** Edmund, second Duke of Somerset, killed at St. Albans (1455), and Henry, his son, killed at Hexham (1464).

87. **hold:** hold its edge; remain powerful.

Striking while the iron is hot. From Claude Menestrier, *L'art des emblemes* (1684).

Oxf. Oxford, Oxford, for Lancaster!

[*He and his forces enter the city.*]

Glou. The gates are open, let us enter too. 70

King Edw. So other foes may set upon our backs.
Stand we in good array; for they no doubt
Will issue out again and bid us battle.
If not, the city being but of small defense,
We'll quickly rouse the traitors in the same. 75

War. O, welcome, Oxford! for we want thy help.

Enter Montagu, with Drum and Colors.

Mon. Montagu, Montagu, for Lancaster!

[*He and his forces enter the city.*]

Glou. Thou and thy brother both shall buy this treason
Even with the dearest blood your bodies bear. 80

King Edw. The harder matched, the greater victory:
My mind presageth happy gain and conquest.

Enter Somerset, with Drum and Colors.

Som. Somerset, Somerset, for Lancaster!

[*He and his forces enter the city.*]

Glou. Two of thy name, both Dukes of Somerset, 85
Have sold their lives unto the house of York;
And thou shalt be the third, if this sword hold.

Enter Clarence, with Drum and Colors.

90. **Of force enough:** supplied with enough men.
99. **trowest thou:** dost thou think.
103. **object:** mention in objection.
105. **Jephthah:** see Judges 11:30–40.

War. And lo where George of Clarence sweeps along,
Of force enough to bid his brother battle; 90
With whom an upright zeal to right prevails
More than the nature of a brother's love!
Come, Clarence, come: thou wilt, if Warwick call.

Clar. Father of Warwick, know you what this means? [*Taking his red rose out of his hat.*] 95
Look, here I throw my infamy at thee.
I will not ruinate my father's house,
Who gave his blood to lime the stones together,
And set up Lancaster. Why, trowest thou, Warwick,
That Clarence is so harsh, so blunt, unnatural, 100
To bend the fatal instruments of war
Against his brother and his lawful king?
Perhaps thou wilt object my holy oath:
To keep that oath were more impiety
Than Jephthah's, when he sacrificed his daughter. 105
I am so sorry for my trespass made
That, to deserve well at my brother's hands,
I here proclaim myself thy mortal foe,
With resolution, wheresoe'er I meet thee—
As I will meet thee, if thou stir abroad— 110
To plague thee for thy foul misleading me.
And so, proud-hearted Warwick, I defy thee
And to my brother turn my blushing cheeks.
Pardon me, Edward, I will make amends.
And, Richard, do not frown upon my faults, 115
For I will henceforth be no more unconstant.

121. **passing:** surpassing; **unjust:** dishonorable.

126. **Barnet:** since Coventry is in Warwickshire, and Barnet is near London, this picture of both armies moving all the way from Coventry to Barnet for their battle is somewhat absurd. Historically, Edward was unable to coax Warwick to come forth and fight and finally moved on to seize London. When Warwick encamped at Barnet, Edward's army engaged him there.

[V.ii.] Edward bears the mortally wounded Warwick from the field and leaves to seek Montagu. Oxford and Somerset find Warwick and tell him that the Queen has brought a power from France. Warwick asks for his brother to take a last farewell and, hearing that he is dead, dies himself. The others set out to join the Queen.

---

3. **bug:** bogey; **feared:** frightened.

King Edw. Now welcome more, and ten times more beloved,
Than if thou never hadst deserved our hate.
Glou. Welcome, good Clarence: this is brother-like. 120
War. O passing traitor, perjured and unjust!
King Edw. What, Warwick, wilt thou leave the town and fight?
Or shall we beat the stones about thine ears?
War. Alas, I am not cooped here for defense! 125
I will away toward Barnet presently
And bid thee battle, Edward, if thou darest.
King Edw. Yes, Warwick, Edward dares and leads the way.
Lords, to the field! St. George and victory! 130
Exeunt [King Edward and his company]. March. Warwick and his company follow.

[Scene II. A field of battle near Barnet.]

Alarum and excursions. Enter King Edward, bringing forth Warwick wounded.

King Edw. So, lie thou there: die thou, and die our fear;
For Warwick was a bug that feared us all.
Now, Montagu, sit fast: I seek for thee,
That Warwick's bones may keep thine company. *Exit.* 5
War. Ah, who is nigh? Come to me, friend or foe,
And tell me, who is victor, York or Warwick?

9. **want:** lack.

14. **ramping:** enraged.

15. **overpeered:** towered over; **Jove's spreading tree:** the oak.

22. **kingly sepulchers:** i.e., because Warwick's displeasure could mean death.

24. **bent his brow:** frowned.

Why ask I that? My mangled body shows,
My blood, my want of strength, my sick heart shows,
That I must yield my body to the earth 10
And, by my fall, the conquest to my foe.
Thus yields the cedar to the ax's edge,
Whose arms gave shelter to the princely eagle,
Under whose shade the ramping lion slept,
Whose top branch overpeered Jove's spreading tree 15
And kept low shrubs from winter's pow'rful wind.
These eyes, that now are dimmed with death's black
veil,
Have been as piercing as the midday sun
To search the secret treasons of the world. 20
The wrinkles in my brows, now filled with blood,
Were likened oft to kingly sepulchers;
For who lived king but I could dig his grave?
And who durst smile when Warwick bent his brow?
Lo, now, my glory smeared in dust and blood! 25
My parks, my walks, my manors that I had,
Even now forsake me, and of all my lands
Is nothing left me but my body's length.
Why, what is pomp, rule, reign, but earth and dust?
And, live we how we can, yet die we must. 30

Enter Oxford and Somerset.

Som. Ah, Warwick, Warwick! wert thou as we are,
We might recover all our loss again.
The Queen from France hath brought a puissant
power:
Even now we heard the news. Ah, couldst thou fly! 35

38. **with thy lips keep in my soul awhile:** i.e., kiss him, to prevent for a while his soul's escape through his mouth.

44. **latest:** last.

45. **Commend me to:** give my greetings to.

48. **mought:** might, could.

[V.iii.] Edward's forces are winning, but, on learning of the Queen's approach with 30,000 men, Edward orders an immediate march to meet them at Tewkesbury.

War. Why, then I would not fly. Ah, Montagu,
If thou be there, sweet brother, take my hand,
And with thy lips keep in my soul awhile!
Thou lovest me not; for, brother, if thou didst,
Thy tears would wash this cold congealed blood 40
That glues my lips and will not let me speak.
Come quickly, Montagu, or I am dead.

Som. Ah, Warwick! Montagu hath breathed his last
And to the latest gasp cried out for Warwick,
And said, "Commend me to my valiant brother." 45
And more he would have said, and more he spoke,
Which sounded like a cannon in a vault,
That mought not be distinguished; but at last
I well might hear, delivered with a groan,
"O, farewell, Warwick!" 50

War. Sweet rest his soul! Fly, lords, and save yourselves;
For Warwick bids you all farewell, to meet in Heaven. [*Dies.*]

Oxf. Away, away, to meet the Queen's great power! 55

Here they bear away his body. Exeunt.

[Scene III. Another part of the field.]

Flourish. Enter King Edward in triumph, with Gloucester, Clarence, and the rest.

King Edw. Thus far our fortune keeps an upward course,

19. **advertised:** informed.

22. **straight:** immediately; **rids way:** makes the way clear.

And we are graced with wreaths of victory.
But, in the midst of this bright-shining day,
I spy a black, suspicious, threat'ning cloud 5
That will encounter with our glorious sun
Ere he attain his easeful western bed:
I mean, my lords, those powers that the Queen
Hath raised in Gallia have arrived our coast,
And, as we hear, march on to fight with us. 10

Clar. A little gale will soon disperse that cloud
And blow it to the source from whence it came.
Thy very beams will dry those vapors up,
For every cloud engenders not a storm.

Glou. The Queen is valued thirty thousand strong, 15
And Somerset, with Oxford, fled to her.
If she have time to breathe, be well assured
Her faction will be full as strong as ours.

King Edw. We are advertised by our loving friends
That they do hold their course toward Tewkesbury. 20
We, having now the best at Barnet field,
Will thither straight, for willingness rids way;
And, as we march, our strength will be augmented
In every county as we go along.
Strike up the drum; cry, "Courage!" and away. 25

Exeunt.

[V.iv.] At Tewkesbury, Queen Margaret, urging her nobles not to be disheartened at the loss of Warwick and Montagu, proposes herself and young Prince Edward as leaders of the Lancastrian army. She points out that deserters will find no mercy at the hands of Edward and his party. Edward exhorts his followers to courage. Both companies prepare for battle.

3. **cheerly:** cheerfully.
7. **Is't meet:** is it suitable.
21. **charge:** responsibility.

[Scene IV. Plains near Tewkesbury.]

Flourish. March. Enter Queen [Margaret, Prince] Edward, Somerset, Oxford, and Soldiers.

Queen M. Great lords, wise men ne'er sit and wail their loss
But cheerly seek how to redress their harms.
What though the mast be now blown overboard,
The cable broke, the holding-anchor lost, 5
And half our sailors swallowed in the flood?
Yet lives our pilot still. Is't meet that he
Should leave the helm and, like a fearful lad,
With tearful eyes add water to the sea,
And give more strength to that which hath too much, 10
Whiles, in his moan, the ship splits on the rock,
Which industry and courage might have saved?
Ah, what a shame! ah, what a fault were this!
Say Warwick was our anchor: what of that?
And Montagu our topmast: what of him? 15
Our slaughtered friends the tackles: what of these?
Why, is not Oxford here another anchor?
And Somerset another goodly mast?
The friends of France our shrouds and tacklings?
And, though unskillful, why not Ned and I 20
For once allowed the skillful pilot's charge?
We will not from the helm to sit and weep,
But keep our course, though the rough wind say no,
From shelves and rocks that threaten us with wrack.

35. **If:** in.
42. **magnanimity:** noble courage.
43. **naked:** unarmed; **foil:** defeat.
46. **betimes:** promptly.

As good to chide the waves as speak them fair. 25
And what is Edward but a ruthless sea?
What Clarence but a quicksand of deceit?
And Richard but a ragged fatal rock?
All these the enemies to our poor bark.
Say you can swim: alas, 'tis but a while! 30
Tread on the sand: why, there you quickly sink.
Bestride the rock: the tide will wash you off:
Or else you famish—that's a threefold death.
This speak I, lords, to let you understand,
If case some one of you would fly from us, 35
That there's no hoped-for mercy with the brothers
More than with ruthless waves, with sands and rocks.
Why, courage then! What cannot be avoided
'Twere childish weakness to lament or fear.
Prince. Methinks a woman of this valiant spirit 10
Should, if a coward heard her speak these words,
Infuse his breast with magnanimity
And make him, naked, foil a man-at-arms.
I speak not this as doubting any here,
For did I but suspect a fearful man, 45
He should have leave to go away betimes,
Lest in our need he might infect another
And make him of like spirit to himself.
If any such be here—as God forbid!—
Let him depart before we need his help. 50
Oxf. Women and children of so high a courage,
And warriors faint! why, 'twere perpetual shame.
O brave young Prince! thy famous grandfather
Doth live again in thee. Long mayst thou live

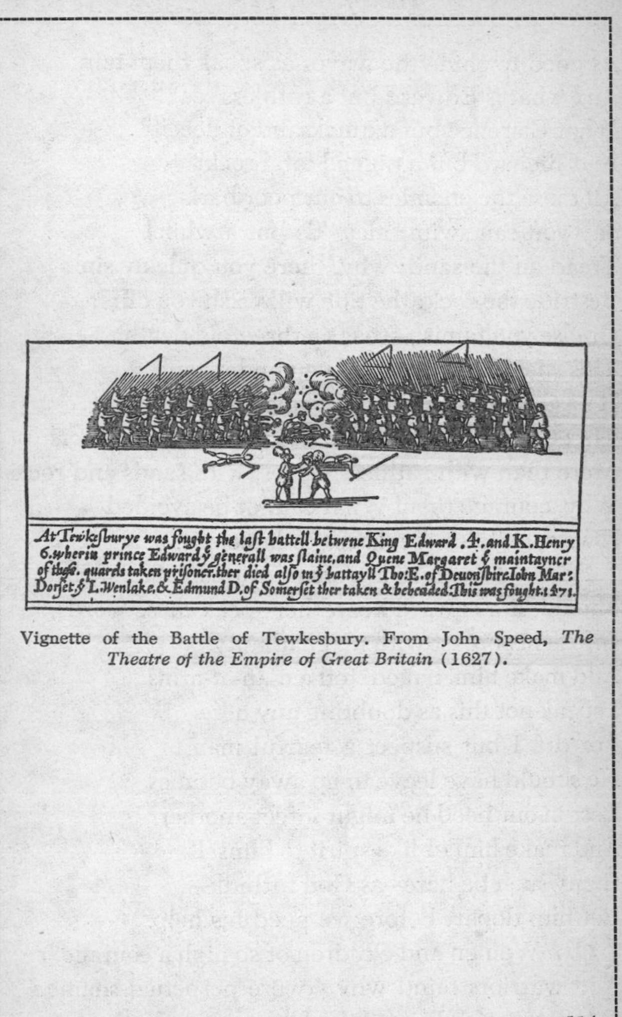

Vignette of the Battle of Tewkesbury. From John Speed, *The Theatre of the Empire of Great Britain* (1627).

To bear his image and renew his glories! 55

Som. And he that will not fight for such a hope,
Go home to bed and, like the owl by day,
If he arisc, bc mocked and wondered at.

Queen M. Thanks, gentle Somerset; sweet Oxford, thanks. 60

Prince. And take his thanks that yet hath nothing else.

Enter a Messenger.

Mess. Prepare you, lords, for Edward is at hand,
Ready to fight: therefore be resolute.

Oxf. I thought no less: it is his policy 65
To haste thus fast, to find us unprovided.

Som. But he's deceived: we are in readiness.

Queen M. This cheers my heart, to see your forwardness.

Oxf. Here pitch our battle. Hence we will not budge. 70

Flourish and March. Enter King Edward, Gloucester, Clarence, and Soldiers.

King Edw. Brave followers, yonder stands the thorny wood
Which, by the Heavens' assistance and your strength,
Must by the roots be hewn up yet ere night.
I need not add more fuel to your fire, 75
For well I wot ye blaze to burn them out.
Give signal to the fight, and to it, lords!

[V.v.] Edward's forces have won the day, and Margaret and her leaders are captives. Prince Edward so enrages King Edward that he stabs the boy, and Gloucester and Clarence also plunge their daggers into him. Margaret, forgetting that Rutland received no greater mercy at Clifford's hands, reproaches them as child murderers and begs them to kill her too. Gloucester, muttering to Clarence about serious business in the Tower, slips away to London. Edward himself sets out for London a little later, hoping that his wife has borne him a son.

---

1. **a period:** an end.

Queen M. Lords, knights, and gentlemen, what I should say
My tears gainsay; for every word I speak, 80
Ye see, I drink the water of my eye.
Therefore, no more but this: Henry, your sovereign,
Is prisoner to the foe, his state usurped,
His realm a slaughterhouse, his subjects slain,
His statutes cancelled, and his treasure spent; 85
And yonder is the wolf that makes this spoil.
You fight in justice: then, in God's name, lords,
Be valiant, and give signal to the fight.

Alarum. Retreat. Excursions. Exeunt.

[Scene V. Another part of the field.]

Flourish. Enter King Edward, Gloucester, Clarence, [*and Soldiers,*] *with Queen Margaret, Oxford, and Somerset,* [*prisoners*].

King Edw. Now here a period of tumultuous broils.
Away with Oxford to Hames Castle straight.
For Somerset, off with his guilty head.
Go, bear them hence: I will not hear them speak.
Oxf. For my part, I'll not trouble thee with words. 5
Som. Nor I, but stoop with patience to my fortune.

Exeunt [*Oxford and Somerset, guarded*].

Queen M. So part we sadly in this troublous world,
To meet with joy in sweet Jerusalem.
King Edw. Is proclamation made that who finds Edward 10

27. **Aesop:** the ancient fabulist, who was reputedly deformed—a hit at Gloucester's own deformity.

28. **currish:** snarling; **sorts not with:** are unbefitting.

37. **malapert:** impudent.

Shall have a high reward, and he his life?

Glou. It is: and lo, where youthful Edward comes!

Enter [Soldiers, with] Prince [Edward].

King Edw. Bring forth the gallant, let us hear him speak.
What! can so young a thorn begin to prick? 15
Edward, what satisfaction canst thou make
For bearing arms, for stirring up my subjects,
And all the trouble thou hast turned me to?

Prince. Speak like a subject, proud ambitious York!
Suppose that I am now my father's mouth: 20
Resign thy chair, and where I stand kneel thou,
Whilst I propose the selfsame words to thee,
Which, traitor, thou wouldst have me answer to.

Queen M. Ah, that thy father had been so resolved!

Glou. That you might still have worn the petticoat 25
And ne'er have stol'n the breech from Lancaster.

Prince. Let Aesop fable in a winter's night:
His currish riddles sorts not with this place.

Glou. By Heaven, brat, I'll plague ye for that word.

Queen M. Ay, thou wast born to be a plague to men. 30

Glou. For God's sake, take away this captive scold.

Prince. Nay, take away this scolding crookback rather.

King Edw. Peace, willful boy, or I will charm your tongue. 35

Clar. Untutored lad, thou art too malapert.

Prince. I know my duty: you are all undutiful.

43–4. **the likeness of this railer here:** i.e., you image of your scolding mother.

65. **by to equal it:** placed alongside for comparison.

66. **respect:** comparison.

Lascivious Edward, and thou perjured George,
And thou misshapen Dick, I tell ye all 40
I am your better, traitors as ye are:
And thou usurpst my father's right and mine.

King Edw. Take that, the likeness of this railer here. *Stabs him.*

Glou. Sprawlst thou? Take that, to end thy agony. 45 *Stabs him.*

Clar. And there's for twitting me with perjury. *Stabs him.*

Queen M. Oh, kill me too!

Glou. Marry, and shall. *Offers to kill her.*

King Edw. Hold, Richard, hold; for we have done too much. 50

Glou. Why should she live, to fill the world with words?

King Edw. What, doth she swoon? Use means for her recovery.

Glou. Clarence, excuse me to the King my brother; 55
I'll hence to London on a serious matter:
Ere ye come there, be sure to hear some news.

Clar. What? what?

Glou. The Tower, the Tower. *Exit.*

Queen M. O Ned, sweet Ned! speak to thy mother, boy! 60
Canst thou not speak? O traitors! murderers!
They that stabbed Caesar shed no blood at all,
Did not offend, nor were not worthy blame,
If this foul deed were by to equal it. 65
He was a man; this, in respect, a child:

77. **rid:** dispatched.
89. **usest to forswear:** are wont to perjure.
92. **Hard-favored:** ugly.
94. **puttest back:** reject.

And men ne'er spend their fury on a child.
What's worse than murderer, that I may name it?
No, no, my heart will burst and if I speak:
And I will speak, that so my heart may burst. 70
Butchers and villains! bloody cannibals!
How sweet a plant have you untimely cropped!
You have no children, butchers! If you had,
The thought of them would have stirred up remorse:
But if you ever chance to have a child, 75
Look in his youth to have him so cut off,
As, deathsmen, you have rid this sweet young Prince!

King Edw. Away with her: go, bear her hence perforce.

Queen M. Nay, never bear me hence, dispatch me here: 80
Here sheathe thy sword, I'll pardon thee my death.
What, wilt thou not? Then, Clarence, do it thou.

Clar. By Heaven, I will not do thee so much ease.

Queen M. Good Clarence, do: sweet Clarence, do thou do it. 85

Clar. Didst thou not hear me swear I would not do it?

Queen M. Ay, but thou usest to forswear thyself.
'Twas sin before, but now 'tis charity. 90
What, wilt thou not? Where is that devil's butcher,
Hard-favored Richard? Richard, where art thou?
Thou art not here: murder is thy alms deed:
Petitioners for blood thou ne'er puttest back.

King Edw. Away, I say; I charge ye, bear her hence. 95

100. **all in post:** riding posthaste.

107. **this:** this time.

[V.vi.] Gloucester arrives at the Tower, where King Henry is imprisoned. The King suspects Gloucester's errand but shows no fear and taunts him until he stirs Gloucester to the murder that he has come to perform. Having killed Henry, Gloucester reveals his plan to get rid of Clarence and one by one all the others who stand in his way to the throne.

5. **"good" was little better:** to call you "good" would be little better than flattering you.

6. **were:** would be.

7. **preposterous:** untrue to a monstrous degree.

Queen M. So come to you and yours as to this Prince! *Exit, [led out forcibly].*

King Edw. Where's Richard gone?

Clar. To London, all in post; and, as I guess, 100
To make a bloody supper in the Tower.

King Edw. He's sudden, if a thing comes in his head.
Now march we hence: discharge the common sort
With pay and thanks and let's away to London 105
And see our gentle queen how well she fares.
By this, I hope, she hath a son for me.

Exeunt.

[Scene VI. London. The Tower.]

Enter King Henry and Gloucester, with the Lieutenant, on the walls.

Glou. Good day, my lord. What, at your book so hard?

King H. Ay, my good lord—my lord, I should say rather.
'Tis sin to flatter; "good" was little better. 5
"Good Gloucester" and "good devil" were alike
And both preposterous: therefore, not "good lord."

Glou. Sirrah, leave us to ourselves: we must confer.

[*Exit Lieutenant.*]

9. **reckless:** heedless (of the safety of his charge).

13. **Roscius:** a famous actor of ancient Rome.

16. **limed in a bush:** trapped in birdlime, which was spread on bushes to catch small birds.

17. **misdoubteth:** suspects.

22. **peevish:** silly; **that of Crete:** referring to the inventor Daedalus, who devised wings so that he and his son, Icarus, could escape from Crete. When Icarus disregarded his father's warning not to fly too high, the sun melted the wax that held his wings in place and he fell into the sea and was drowned.

23. **office:** function (i.e., flight).

24. **fool:** punning on "fowl."

26. **Minos:** King of Crete, who had imprisoned Daedalus.

29. **envious:** hostile.

32. **history:** tale.

Icarus and Daedalus. From Jean Baudoin, *Recueil d'emblemes divers* (1638-39).

King H. So flies the reckless shepherd from the wolf; 10
So first the harmless sheep doth yield his fleece
And next his throat unto the butcher's knife.
What scene of death hath Roscius now to act?
Glou. Suspicion always haunts the guilty mind;
The thief doth fear each bush an officer. 15
King H. The bird that hath been limed in a bush,
With trembling wings misdoubteth every bush;
And I, the hapless male to one sweet bird,
Have now the fatal object in my eye
Where my poor young was limed, was caught and killed. 20
Glou. Why, what a peevish fool was that of Crete
That taught his son the office of a fowl!
And yet, for all his wings, the fool was drowned.
King H. I, Daedalus; my poor boy, Icarus; 25
Thy father, Minos, that denied our course;
The sun that seared the wings of my sweet boy,
Thy brother Edward, and thyself the sea
Whose envious gulf did swallow up his life.
Ah, kill me with thy weapon, not with words! 30
My breast can better brook thy dagger's point
Than can my ears that tragic history.
But wherefore dost thou come? Is't for my life?
Glou. Thinkst thou I am an executioner?
King H. A persecutor, I am sure, thou art. 35
If murdering innocents be executing,
Why, then thou art an executioner.
Glou. Thy son I killed for his presumption.

43. **mistrust no parcel of my fear:** do not share my fear.

45. **water-standing:** tearful.

47. **timeless:** untimely.

50. **aboding luckless time:** boding an evil future time.

52. **rooked her:** crouched herself. The raven was also considered an ominous bird.

53. **pies:** magpies.

56. **indigested:** shapeless.

58. **Teeth hadst thou . . . when thou wast born:** John Rous, in his chronicle entitled *Historia regum Angliae* (*ca.* 1490), described Richard as possessing teeth at birth.

King H. Hadst thou been killed when first thou didst presume, 40
Thou hadst not lived to kill a son of mine.
And thus I prophesy: that many a thousand,
Which now mistrust no parcel of my fear,
And many an old man's sigh and many a widow's,
And many an orphan's water-standing eye— 45
Men for their sons, wives for their husbands,
And orphans for their parents' timeless death—
Shall rue the hour that ever thou wast born.
The owl shrieked at thy birth—an evil sign;
The night crow cried, aboding luckless time; 50
Dogs howled, and hideous tempest shook down trees;
The raven rooked her on the chimney's top;
And chatt'ring pies in dismal discords sung.
Thy mother felt more than a mother's pain,
And yet brought forth less than a mother's hope, 55
To wit, an indigested and deformed lump,
Not like the fruit of such a goodly tree.
Teeth hadst thou in thy head when thou wast born,
To signify thou camest to bite the world:
And, if the rest be true which I have heard, 60
Thou camest—
Glou. I'll hear no more: die, prophet, in thy speech.
Stabs him.
For this, amongst the rest, was I ordained.
King H. Ay, and for much more slaughter after this.
Oh, God forgive my sins and pardon thee! *Dies.* 65
Glou. What, will the aspiring blood of Lancaster
Sink in the ground? I thought it would have mounted.

74. **that:** what.

90. **sort a pitchy day:** select a day of misfortune.

91. **buzz abroad such prophecies:** in the first scene of *Richard III*, Clarence is under arrest because of prophecies that one "G" would be responsible for the death of King Edward's heirs. "G," of course, could stand for "George" or "Gloucester."

See how my sword weeps for the poor King's death!
Oh, may such purple tears be always shed
From those that wish the downfall of our house! 70
If any spark of life be yet remaining,
Down, down to hell; and say I sent thee thither:
Stabs him again.
I, that have neither pity, love, nor fear.
Indeed, 'tis true that Henry told me of,
For I have often heard my mother say 75
I came into the world with my legs forward.
Had I not reason, think ye, to make haste
And seek their ruin that usurped our right?
The midwife wondered, and the women cried,
"Oh, Jesus bless us, he is born with teeth!" 80
And so I was; which plainly signified
That I should snarl and bite and play the dog.
Then, since the Heavens have shaped my body so,
Let hell make crook'd my mind to answer it.
I have no brother, I am like no brother; 85
And this word "love," which graybeards call divine,
Be resident in men like one another
And not in me: I am myself alone.
Clarence, beware; thou keepst me from the light:
But I will sort a pitchy day for thee; 90
For I will buzz abroad such prophecies
That Edward shall be fearful of his life,
And then, to purge his fear, I'll be thy death.
King Henry and the Prince his son are gone:
Clarence, thy turn is next, and then the rest, 95
Counting myself but bad till I be best.

[**V.vii.**] Edward, newly reseated on the throne, expresses his content at having overcome all the threats to his security and that of his heir, young Prince Edward. Gloucester and Clarence show outward love and duty, but Gloucester is only biding his time. When Clarence inquires what should be done with Margaret, whose father has paid a ransom for her, Edward orders her shipped off to France. He decrees festive celebrations of his success and dismisses all thought of further trouble.

3. **Repurchased:** regained.
5. **tops:** the height.
8. **as:** namely.
10. **coursers:** war horses.
11. **bears:** referring to the emblem of the bear and ragged staff borne by their family.
15. **swept suspicion from our seat:** dispelled all fear that our seat on the throne might be shaken.
16. **made our footstool of security:** made security our footstool. This may contain a typically Shakespearean irony: **security** was often used in a sense implying false confidence. Edward's real security is not to last long.
19. **watched:** remained sleepless.

I'll throw thy body in another room,
And triumph, Henry, in thy day of doom.
Exit, [with the body].

[Scene VII. London. The palace.]

Flourish. Enter King [Edward], Queen [Elizabeth], Clarence, Gloucester, Hastings, a Nurse [with the young Prince], and Attendants.

King Edw. Once more we sit in England's royal throne,
Repurchased with the blood of enemies.
What valiant foemen, like to autumn's corn,
Have we mowed down in tops of all their pride! 5
Three dukes of Somerset, threefold renowned
For hardy and undoubted champions;
Two Cliffords, as, the father and the son;
And two Northumberlands—two braver men
Ne'er spurred their coursers at the trumpet's sound— 10
With them, the two brave bears, Warwick and Montagu,
That in their chains fettered the kingly lion
And made the forest tremble when they roared.
Thus have we swept suspicion from our seat 15
And made our footstool of security.
Come hither, Bess, and let me kiss my boy.
Young Ned, for thee, thine uncles and myself
Have in our armors watched the winter's night,

23–4. **if your head were laid:** i.e., once you are leveled in death.

25. **looked on:** regarded with due respect.

40. **whenas:** when.

47. **it:** the money secured by pawning the Sicilies and Jerusalem.

The kiss of Judas. From Gabriel Chappuys, *Figures de la Bible* (1582).

Went all afoot in summer's scalding heat, 20
That thou mightst repossess the crown in peace;
And of our labors thou shalt reap the gain.
Glou. [*Aside*] I'll blast his harvest, if your head were laid;
For yet I am not looked on in the world. 25
This shoulder was ordained so thick to heave;
And heave it shall some weight, or break my back.
Work thou the way—and thou shalt execute.
King Edw. Clarence and Gloucester, love my lovely queen; 30
And kiss your princely nephew, brothers both.
Clar. The duty that I owe unto your Majesty
I seal upon the lips of this sweet babe.
Queen E. Thanks, noble Clarence, worthy brother, thanks. 35
Glou. And, that I love the tree from whence thou sprangst,
Witness the loving kiss I give the fruit.
[*Aside*] To say the truth, so Judas kissed his Master,
And cried, "All hail!" whenas he meant all harm. 40
King Edw. Now am I seated as my soul delights,
Having my country's peace and brothers' loves.
Clar. What will your Grace have done with Margaret?
Reignier, her father, to the King of France 45
Hath pawned the Sicils and Jerusalem,
And hither have they sent it for her ransom.
King Edw. Away with her and waft her hence to France.
And now what rests but that we spend the time 50

51. **triumphs:** festive spectacles.
53. **sour annoy:** bitter injury.

With stately triumphs, mirthful comic shows,
Such as befits the pleasure of the court?
Sound drums and trumpets! Farewell sour annoy!
For here, I hope, begins our lasting joy.

Exeunt omnes.

KEY TO

Famous Lines

Do but think
How sweet a thing it is to wear a crown,
Within whose circuit is Elysium
And all that poets feign of bliss and joy.
[*Gloucester*—I.ii.30–3]

Now Phaëthon hath tumbled from his car
And made an evening at the noontide prick.
[*Clifford*—I.iv.33–4]

I will not bandy with thee word for word
But buckler with thee blows, twice two for one.
[*Clifford*—I.iv.49–50]

She-wolf of France, but worse than wolves of France,
Whose tongue more poisons than the adder's tooth!
[*York*—I.iv.115–17]

O tiger's heart wrapped in a woman's hide!
[*York*—I.iv.143]

See how the morning opes her golden gates
And takes her farewell of the glorious sun!
How well resembles it the prime of youth,
Trimmed like a younker, prancing to his love!
[*Gloucester*—II.i.21–4]

Environed he was with many foes
And stood against them, as the hope of Troy
Against the Greeks that would have entered Troy.
But Hercules himself must yield to odds;
And many strokes, though with a little ax,
Hews down and fells the hardest-timbered oak.
[*Messenger*—II.i.53–8]

The smallest worm will turn, being trodden on;
And doves will peck in safeguard of their brood.
[*Clifford*—II.ii.19–20]

This battle fares like to the morning's war,
When dying clouds contend with growing light.
[*Henry*—II.v.1–2]

O God! methinks it were a happy life
To be no better than a homely swain; . . .
[*Henry*—II.v.21–54]

Why, I can smile, and murder whiles I smile, . . .
[*Gloucester*—III.ii.234–47]

If secret powers
Suggest but truth to my divining thoughts,
This pretty lad will prove our country's bliss.
[*Henry*—IV.vi.75–7]

When the fox hath once got in his nose,
He'll soon find means to make the body follow.
[*Gloucester*—IV.vii.30–2]

What, will the aspiring blood of Lancaster
Sink in the ground? I thought it would have mounted.
[*Gloucester*—V.vi.66–7]

I have no brother, I am like no brother;
And this word "love," which graybeards call divine,
Be resident in men like one another
And not in me: I am myself alone.
[*Gloucester*—V.vi.85–8]